Fundamentals of Adopting the NIST Cybersecurity Framework

Volume 1 of the
**Create, Protect, and Deliver
Digital Business Value** series

Published by TSO (The Stationery Office), part of Williams Lea,
www.tsoshop.co.uk

Mail, Telephone, Fax & Email
TSO
PO Box 29, Norwich, NR3 1GN
Telephone orders/General enquiries: 0333 202 5070
Fax orders: 0333 202 5080
Email: customer.services@tso.co.uk
Textphone 0333 202 5077
www.tsoshop.co.uk

DVMS Institute LLC
742 Mink Ave., #135
Murrells Inlet, SC 29576
Phone (401) 764-0721
www.dvmsinstitute.com

Copyright © DVMS Institute LLC 2022

Authors: David Moskowitz and David M. Nichols

Subject Matter Expert and Chief Examiner: David Moskowitz

The rights of David Nichols and David Moskowitz to be identified as the authors of this work/materials and anything contained in this publication have been asserted by them in accordance with the Copyright, Designs and Patents Act 1988 (as amended) and any applicable laws in the United States of America and worldwide; all rights remain reserved by the authors.

Notice of Rights/Restricted Rights
All rights reserved. Reproduction or transmittal of this work/materials and anything contained in this publication or any portion thereof by any means whatsoever without prior written permission of the DVMS Institute LLC is strictly prohibited. No title or ownership of this work/materials and anything contained in this publication, or any portion thereof, or its contents is transferred or assigned, and any use of the work/materials and anything contained in this package or any portion thereof beyond the terms of any license, is strictly forbidden unless the prior written authorization of the DVMS Institute LLC is obtained in advance and in writing.

Notice of Liability
The contents in this work/materials and anything contained in this publication is distributed "As Is," without warranty of any kind, either express or implied, including but not limited to implied warranties for its quality, performance, merchantability, or fitness for any particular purpose. Neither the authors, the DVMS Institute, nor the publisher, its employees, agents, dealers and/or distributors shall be liable to any end user(s) or third parties with respect to any liability, loss and/or damage caused and/or alleged to have been caused directly and/or indirectly by the contents of this material or any parts thereof, and the aforementioned parties disclaim all such representations and warranties and assume no responsibility for any errors, inaccuracies, omissions, or any other inconsistencies herein.

The publication may include hyperlinks to third-party content, advertising and websites, provided for the sake of convenience and interest. Neither the authors, the DVMS Institute, nor the publisher endorse any advertising and/or products available from external sources or third parties.

Trademarks
DVMS Institute LLC is a trademark of DVMS Institute LLC, and all original content is © Copyright DVMS Institute LLC. itSM Solutions LLC is a trademark of itSM Solutions LLC. NCSP® is a registered trademark of CySec Professionals Ltd. Other product names mentioned in this package may be trademarks or registered trademarks of their respective companies and/or owners/authors.

If you have any feedback that you would like to record in our change control log, please send this to
commissioning@williamslea.com

First edition (2022)
ISBN 9780117093706

Contents

Foreword

Cybersecurity is a fundamental problem that affects virtually every person and organization worldwide. To deal with the threats, vulnerabilities, and concomitant risks, organizations need a holistic approach to identify and prioritize their needs. The NIST Cybersecurity Framework (NIST-CSF) helps organizations to manage complex problems by using a common business language (Identify, Protect, Detect, Respond, and Recover; NIST, 2018) to assess their capabilities, identify gaps, and prioritize cybersecurity investments.

The purpose of this guidance is to help people engage in this conversation. By helping businesses to align and prioritize their governance with cyber risk, they improve their strategic capabilities, create more adaptive, flexible organizations, and prepare themselves to compete successfully in the marketplace. In any market situation, there are competitive challenges, key alternatives, and difficult decisions to make. Business stakeholders are actively embracing digital business models, which enable them to serve new or existing customers in fundamentally different ways. This creates meaningful opportunities for additional revenue, improved profitability, and reduced costs. But to achieve these business objectives, they must be able to achieve them safely.

This book helps you to better assess organizational strategic goals, the role of cyber risk management in achieving those goals, and the specific approaches to help you balance risk and reward. The NIST-CSF is one such approach when considering the practice disciplines and business outcomes that a successful cybersecurity risk management program must provide. By using the Framework to assess organizational capabilities, engage in a risk assessment, and prioritize gaps, you will be able to help your organization optimize its cybersecurity investments and produce the most optimized result.

The CPD Model outlined in this guide will help your organization to build a functioning roadmap for assessing your capabilities, establishing your objectives, and beginning an ongoing journey to improve your cybersecurity risk capabilities. More importantly, these practices are critical in helping your organization to achieve its digital business goals and ensure competitiveness. I have had the privilege of working directly with the authors for many years, and I am constantly impressed by the pragmatism of their approach – no bells, no whistles, just practical advice that your organization can adopt and adapt to its needs.

I strongly recommend this book for any organization wrestling with the practical challenges of balancing stakeholders' value creation needs with value protection. Enjoy the book, and I hope to engage with many of you as you continue on your journey in managing strategy and risk.

Good luck!

Patrick von Schlag
President, Deep Creek Center
NIST cybersecurity specialist and lead trainer

Preface

Before we knew each other, the evolution of thought for this three-volume series (aptly named "Create, Protect, and Deliver Digital Business Value") occurred when we independently read the first edition of Peter Senge's *The Fifth Discipline* (Senge, 1990). Senge's book coalesced years of thinking about technology and business for each of us. The specific genesis of the series dates back to 2011 when we started collaborating on developing courses and related material about IT service management. Over the years, our thinking about IT service management systems merged with ideas related to cyber-resilience, and our thinking matured into a value-based scheme. We asked questions about why current approaches to cyber-resilience failed. This thinking led to creating a unified model that rationalized the relationships and interactions of the business, IT, and cybersecurity.

At about the same time (2014), President Obama signed an executive order that directed the National Institute of Standards and Technology (NIST) to create a cybersecurity framework that the nation's critical infrastructure sectors could adopt to provide more robust cybersecurity capabilities. The NIST Cybersecurity Framework (NIST-CSF) achieved widespread adoption in the US and abroad. However, it gives only "what and why" guidance; it does not cover "how." Organizations wishing to adopt the Framework must figure out how to adapt its guidance. The books in this series represent our approach to the question, "How do we make adopting and adapting the Framework easier?"

In the meantime, headlines about the latest high-profile cybersecurity breaches impacting commercial and governmental agencies kept recurring. We thought the common thread that ran through most of these high-profile breaches was *not* a technology failure but a failure of business leadership – including the notion that compliance meant protection. Cybersecurity is not an IT problem solved by buying more hardware or software, nor simply complying with relevant standards – even adding cybersecurity professionals hasn't solved the challenges. Cybersecurity is a business problem that starts with the most senior organizational leadership and filters down through the organization to its lowest levels.

The idea for this series crystallized when one of the authors asked a well-known and respected cybersecurity expert, "What happens when you hand in your cybersecurity assessment report?" The answer was stunning: "I don't know." This response bothered us, individually and collectively, but why? What was wrong with this picture?

The short answer is that the board was ticking a checkbox by commissioning a cybersecurity assessment. The C-level folks gave it to the IT folks. When the IT folks asked for money to close the reported gaps, there were no available funds outside the regular IT budget. At their very best, the IT folks could only "bolt-on" as many cybersecurity resources as they could afford, without going to the nub of the problem.

This series addresses the complex issue of managing cybersecurity risk. It will take you on a journey, the first part of which prepares an organization to adopt the NIST-CSF, including introducing you to our unified model. It covers what you need to know before starting. The central message of all three books is: To adopt a paradigm, you will need a different mindset, one that focuses on creating, protecting, and delivering digital business value to stakeholders. You will learn to treat value creation and value protection as different sides of the same coin, because unprotected value has no value.

The required paradigm shift starts by making cybersecurity an inseparable aspect of strategy, which is the focus of the first book in the series. It is also the responsibility of the most senior management in the boardroom and C-suite (or comparable military or governmental leadership hierarchy). Understanding cybersecurity risk and incorporating it into the organizational strategy are essential aspects of ensuring that your business succeeds in today's competitive marketplace.

Enjoy the journey!

David Moskowitz, *Executive Director for Content Development, DVMS Institute LLC*

David Nichols, *Executive Director, DVMS Institute LLC*

About the authors

David Moskowitz

David is the content architect of the DVMS Institute. In this role, he actively looks for and works with subject matter experts to develop relevant content for the institute.

David started his formal career as an operating systems programmer and systems architect, before going on to look at different forms of systems and complexity while serving in the US Army. After his military service, he continued to apply a systems approach to his job, working on an anti-submarine warfare program for the US Department of Defense. By applying a whole-systems perspective, he addressed organizational and inter-personal issues and created a high-performing team.

The team stumbled into an approach that today many people would recognize as parts of IT service management and Kanban. It included a formalized approach to managing change, combined with incremental development performed in short iterations that received constant feedback. Later, as a consultant, he assisted organizations in adopting what they considered to be technical disruptions, applying a critical lesson learned from experience: "Every problem was, at its core, a people problem, not a technology problem." Technology was either an enabler or an inhibitor. The recurring mantra of these efforts was, "Solve the problem; don't treat the symptom."

David first met Dave Nichols in 2008, and since then they have worked together to develop a systems approach to accelerate the creation and delivery of business value. David views cybersecurity as a critical aspect of quality and value.

David thanks his wife Rosemary for her patience, tolerance and encouragement, without whom this book would not have been possible. He can be contacted at david.moskowitz@dvmsinstitute.com; for more information, visit www.dvmsinstitute.com.

David Nichols

Dave is the executive director of the DVMS Institute. The institute's mission is to enable organizations to create, protect, and deliver digital business value through a curated portfolio of content and programs that bring value to its member stakeholders. Dave's role is to work with the industry's leading practitioners in risk management, service management, cybersecurity, assurance, and business leadership to produce industry-leading guidance and programs that will enable organizations to survive and thrive in a digital business world.

Dave spent his formative years on US Navy submarines, where he gained his knowledge of complex systems and how to function in high-performance teams. He took these skills into civilian life, where he built a successful career in software development and service delivery.

In 2000, Dave formed itSM Solutions with his partners, Janet Kuhn and Rick Lemieux, to create and deliver service management certification training and consulting programs to Fortune 500 companies. In 2015, his team created the award-winning APMG-accredited NIST Cybersecurity Professional (NCSP®) training scheme, which teaches organizations how to rapidly engineer and operationalize a cybersecurity risk management program. Dave also oversaw the certification of the NCSP program by the National Cyber Security Centre in the UK and its listing as a qualified training scheme by the US Department of Homeland Security's CISA organization.

Dave would like to thank Zelda, his wife of more than 50 years, for her support and inspiration when it was needed most. He can be contacted at david.nichols@dvmsinstitute.com; for more information, visit www.dvmsinstitute.com.

Acknowledgments

DVMS Institute and TSO kindly thank those who participated in the review process:

Roy Atkinson, CEO, Clifton Butterfield LLC

Michael Battistella, President, Solutions³ LLC

Ian W. Daykin, entrepreneur and business consultant

Bradley Laatsch, HPE education delivery manager, Hewlett Packard Enterprise

Rick Lemieux, co-founder and executive director of programs, DVMS Institute

Greg Sanker, former CIO, author and speaker

Patrick von Schlag, President, Deep Creek Center

This book is dedicated to Janet Kuhn, a generalist and a specialist, our special generalist.

CHAPTER 1

Looking through the wrong end of the telescope

1 Looking through the wrong end of the telescope

"To change ourselves effectively, we first had to change our perceptions."
Stephen R. Covey (2004)

It's too complex. It's too costly. It's a technical problem – let the IT department handle it. This new tool will solve ... and the list goes on.

Have you heard these statements? Did you guess we're talking about cybersecurity?

Many organizations faced with real-life cybersecurity challenges look through the telescope from the wrong end. What they see is a small part of the whole. Cybersecurity isn't the problem. The problem with cybersecurity is twofold: the first problem is one of perception; the second results from looking through the telescope incorrectly – in other words, it is a failure to see the whole.

Instead of approaching cybersecurity from an enterprise level, the organization relegates it to the IT department. Then it asks the wrong questions about cybersecurity – as if it were a piece of hardware or software – for example, "How much will this cost?"

Another aspect of this wrong-end-of-the-telescope perspective is that the organization approaches value creation for stakeholders by focusing on profit or revenue targets. The idea of cybersecurity being a technical problem and stakeholder value being dependent on money demonstrates a failure to approach value from the perspective of stakeholders versus the bottom line – an additional way to look through the wrong end of the telescope.

When an organization provides or produces something of genuine value for its stakeholders, it's a certainty that there will be someone who tries either to access, change, steal, or sell it, deprive the organization of its use, or worse. This "thing" of value may not be obvious; for example, the convenience of credit card processing. It could be fuel through a pipeline or patient records. The point, however, is that if it has value to you or your stakeholders, then it has value to "them."

"It is not necessary to change. Survival is not mandatory."
W. Edwards Deming

We need to change the mental model associated with cybersecurity from a technical challenge to one that considers cybersecurity to be essential to value production. This change in perception is the magic bullet to address these issues – but it is not easy.

The best way to approach creating a different mental model is to ask different questions. Ask questions that focus on creating and protecting value:

- What is valuable to us?
- What is valuable to our stakeholders?
- How is that value protected?
- Are we prepared to respond when something compromises any aspect of value?

If the organization doesn't proactively take appropriate steps to protect that value, does it provide value? Another way to ask this question is this: If the value we deliver doesn't have appropriate protections for value-stakeholders, is it still valuable to them?

One of the themes you'll see repeated throughout this book is that value creation and value protection are two different sides of the same coin. It's essential to do both: value *must* be protected at an appropriate level for the organization, understanding that value changes over time. Cybersecurity *is* an intrinsic aspect of business value.

The idea of a shift in perception is associated with another theme: the need to apply systems thinking, which views cybersecurity as an enterprise responsibility, and not that of a single department (or similar internal organizational unit).

1.1   For NIST Cybersecurity Professional (NCSP) students

The material in this book provides the rubric for the NCSP Foundation course. It presents the narrative that accompanies your course material. The book contains more information than will fit into the course. Consequently, we recommend that you read the whole book instead of focusing on just the material in the syllabus.

If you understand the flow of the story in this book, it will be easier to pass the course examination.

1.2   Using the book

The key to adopting and applying systems thinking when dealing with complex problems is to look at the system as a "whole" (rather than a "hole") and to develop an innate understanding of its components and behaviors. This approach to creating and protecting value concurrently requires you to understand the existing threat landscape. It also requires you to understand how the threat landscape evolves with technology. You'll find this material in **Chapter 2**.

Another "different" aspect to consider when developing new mental models is the assumption linking cybersecurity with technology. "How should we position cybersecurity outside of IT?" There's an answer in history. In his 1985 book *Innovation and Entrepreneurship*, Peter Drucker wrote: "Customers pay for what is of use to them and gives them value. Nothing else constitutes 'quality.'" (Drucker, 1985). In **Chapter 3**, you'll find a discussion about the link between quality and value explored in the context of the model we've created, called the *CPD Model* (CPD being an abbreviation for "creating, protecting, and delivering" digital business value). This chapter also discusses how to determine what to protect and how much protection is needed. What is the risk to the organization if …? These questions require applying a principled approach to enterprise risk management (ERM).

Chapter 4 presents our approach to adopting the NIST Framework for Improving Critical Infrastructure Cybersecurity (NIST-CSF). Although you can jump directly to that chapter, we recommend reading Chapters 2 and 3 first. Doing so will make it easier to apply the NIST-CSF discussion.

Chapter 5 presents a more detailed discussion of the CPD Model that is briefly introduced in Chapter 3. It provides an overlay for any organization desiring to apply the new concept to link business value creation with its protection. The model presents a view of this system of systems, presented in the context of the NIST-CSF. This approach makes it easier to understand how to adopt the NIST-CSF and adapt it to fit the organizational need.

Every organization represents a potentially complex system – in effect, a system of systems – from a single-person company to a multinational enterprise (including government and military entities). Among the many things it must do, it must manage stakeholders, produce something, move things or people, communicate, provide accounts payable and receivables, etc. Each of these represents a "subsystem" of the whole. The core capability of adapting to a dynamic environment means that this system of systems must continually adapt to seek an equilibrium that optimizes the likelihood of survival.

"[A] mind, once stretched by a new idea, never regains its original dimensions."
Oliver Wendell Holmes Sr.

Think about this quotation. Now consider this: *Once an organization sees the "whole" and understands that value drives its adaptation to its environment, it can't "unsee" it.* "Seeing" enables the organization to change its perception of strategy and risk. Risk is an intrinsic aspect of strategy, creating a single entity: *strategy-risk*. Strategy-risk is a concept that subsumes creating value as part of what it takes to protect and deliver business value.

As noted above, Drucker linked value with quality. From this perspective, the only way to deliver value is to change the perception of cybersecurity from a technical challenge to an organizational requirement. Everyone is responsible for quality, not just the IT department.

Viewed from this perspective, as the perception of value changes, so does the perception of quality. It requires the organization to see the enterprise as a whole, not as isolated or disparate parts. The idea of seeing the whole is a crucial aspect of systems thinking.

There's more to adopting the NIST-CSF than the mere framework. The material in **Chapter 6** introduces a holistic approach to understanding what comes next. The chapter addresses the core point that cybersecurity is not a technical problem – it's an enterprise problem. The board of directors (or equivalent governing body) must accept responsibility and be held accountable for cybersecurity.

Nearly every aspect of an organization has some digital dependency; therefore every organization has to figure out how to create and protect digital business value. Accepting this point of view lays the foundation for adopting and adapting the NIST-CSF.

When value or quality changes, it stands to reason that the organization must change along with it. The idea that change is constant is not new. The concepts of stability and change are not mutually exclusive, yet many organizations seek stasis in place of stability. At its core, a stable organization can adapt to change by evolving internal needs, external requirements, and the threat environment.

How an organization perceives cybersecurity is shaped by its leadership and normalized in its culture. In too many cases, perception is achieved by looking through the wrong end of a telescope. The problem with cybersecurity is not about cybersecurity; it's about the perception of cybersecurity.

"I am not crazy; my reality is just different from yours."
Cheshire Cat in Alice in Wonderland (Lewis Carroll)

1.3   The rest of the story

This book provides a practical approach to adopting the NIST-CSF.

The second book provides more detailed information for the practitioner and the specialist. It covers the following topics:

- Developing a deep understanding of the threat landscape to be proactive
- Dealing with complexity
- Cybersecurity and the Digital Value Management System (DVMS)

- An adaptive way of working
- Cybersecurity within a system
- Strategy-risk: creating, protecting, and delivering digital business value
- Innovation for effect
- Overview of the DVMS.

The first two books focus on cybersecurity and introduce the DVMS as an overlay. The third book presents the DVMS as an enabler for an adaptive, cyber-resilient organization. It describes a scalable way for any organization to treat value creation and value protection as aspects of quality, regardless of size.

The three books will help you to recognize when you are looking through the wrong end of the telescope.

Fundamentals of Adopting the NIST Cybersecurity Framework

CHAPTER 2

A clear and present danger

2 A clear and present danger

> *"There is nothing new in the world except the history you do not know."*
> Harry S Truman, 33rd President of the US

The danger is real. Threat actors use anything and everything to seek an advantage. It could be something they find on your website, an article or paper about the organization, an interview, a podcast, anything. If it gives them an edge, they use it.

Threat actors exploit vulnerabilities in people, processes, and technology. As the organizational digital footprint expands, so does the resulting attack surface – and the risk is not just associated with technology. As the surface expands, the complexity increases, impacting people and processes. It's all linked.

Consider the following statement: "If it has value to you, no matter how small the perceived value might be, then it has value to them." As the digital footprint and capability expand, so does the associated risk and the need for increased protection, to the point that it's become an ongoing escalating digital warfare. Consider this breach described by the FBI at the 2019 Cybersecurity Summit in Philadelphia, PA, US, to make the point.

> *"Hackers exfiltrated data from several job posting/résumé sites. The same nefarious group scanned for new hires on various company websites. They used the information to craft effective phishing attacks when they found a match between the exfiltrated résumé data and someone recently hired at a target organization."*

Think about this set of attacks from two perspectives. The first perspective is the creativity of these *bad actors.*[1] They obtained information to improve their phishing attacks. They targeted young new hires who had not had the opportunity to complete the onboarding, including cybersecurity training. This type of attack doesn't happen by accident. Threat actors experiment; if one thing doesn't work, they try something else. They keep learning and improving their techniques to penetrate target organizations.

The second perspective is the breadth and depth of the threat landscape, which represents the totality of all potential lanes of attack by threat actors, including vulnerability exploitation and malware. It also includes groups of attackers and their techniques and advanced persistent threats (APTs). An APT is usually a nation-state or a nation-state-sponsored group (Wikipedia, 2021a).

The threat landscape is much broader than the vulnerabilities associated with a direct attack. In the example above, bad actors collected data from one company website to improve their attacks on another. There is also a much more public example of an indirect attack: SolarWinds. In this case, the bad actors planted malware in SolarWinds' Orion software system, distributed to clients on demand. Think about the insidious nature of this attack; if that doesn't get your attention, what will?

---

1   We use the terms *bad actors, malicious actors*, and *threat actors* interchangeably to refer to entities responsible for a cybersecurity incident that impacts (or has the potential to impact) organizational security.

Initially, threat actors focused on attacking technology, for example, a buffer overflow and SQL injection. Today, malicious actors concentrate on attacking the weakest link: people.[2] Their attacks might be partially indirect to achieve their nefarious goals. Consider the episode mentioned above. The bad actors infiltrated a résumé site to gather intelligence to improve the attack on the target organization.

Then consider another form of indirect attack: the SolarWinds attack. Here, the malicious actors used the supply chain to infect multiple targets. SolarWinds wasn't the target – its customers were. Later in this chapter are other examples of an indirect attack where attackers breached vendors to access their primary objective.

How did we get from simple anti-virus software being sufficient to where we are now – potentially needing multiple cybersecurity tools and teams of people? To appreciate the answers to this question, we need to explore how digital capabilities evolved with the corresponding evolution of digital threats.

2.1   Digital evolution and the expanding attack surface[3]

The tendency is to believe digital transformation is a new concept. It's not. It follows a trend that started in the 1950s and continues today. Every piece of technology we enjoy today evolved from ideas, implementations, and products decades in the making.

"Overnight success stories take a long time."
Steve Jobs, co-founder of Apple Computer

2.1.1   The beginnings of modern-day computing

Let's start with an abbreviated computer hardware history – from vacuum tubes to very large-scale integration (VLSI) and beyond.

In 1952, the UNIVAC 1 created a buzz when it correctly predicted the US presidential election with a sample size of less than 6% of the total vote (Wikipedia, 2021h). The UNIVAC 1 was a primitive vacuum tube-based computer compared with current computing. It was a first-generation computer[4] that could do only one thing, one program at a time; it was a dedicated computer – dedicated to a single task or program at a time. As illustrated in Figure 2.1, every program required code to interact directly with the computer hardware – in effect, each program "owned" the computer.

---

2   Technology vulnerabilities are still exploited, including zero-day attacks, covered in more detail later in this chapter.
3   This section does not provide an exhaustive and complete history of modern computing. It provides a historical context to understand the digital evolution and the associated impact on the broader attack surfaces.
4   UNIVAC (Universal Automatic Computer) was the world's first commercially produced electronic digital computer. https://www.history.com/this-day-in-history/univac-computer-dedicated

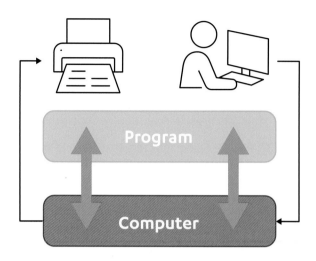

Figure 2.1 Application "code" talking directly to computer hardware

Transistors[5] replaced vacuum tubes in commercial computing in the late 1950s into the 1960s, and ushered in the second generation of computing. These computers were smaller, faster, and cooler (i.e., they generated less heat).

Instead of dedicated computing, computer manufacturers developed operating systems that meant applications did not need to talk directly to the computer hardware. Instead, the applications used libraries of functions built into the operating system (e.g., a simple PRINT command versus the more detailed requirements of the first-generation computers that required the application to "talk" directly to the printer).

The advent of operating systems allowed application developers to focus on a specific problem without the code needed to control the computer hardware. Instead of hard-coded instructions to talk directly to the computer hardware, the operating system provided an abstraction layer that hid the hardware complexity from the applications developers (see Figure 2.2).

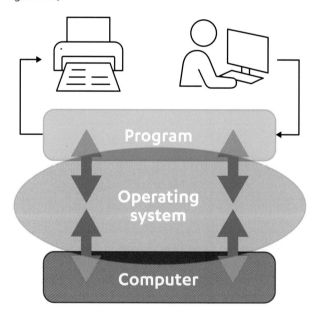

Figure 2.2 Application program run on top of an operating system that talked to hardware

---

5 Transistors were invented in 1947 at Bell Labs and were the start of a family of components called semiconductors (Wikipedia, 2021g).

The combination of transistors and the evolution of the operating systems is part of the second generation of computing. At the same time, operating systems reduced the complexity involved with creating applications programs, and they also introduced additional complexity to the computing process.[6]

The third generation was based on monolithic integrated circuits, invented in 1959. The most widely known third-generation computer was the IBM/360 Model 85 (1969); the technology was used extensively in the IBM/370 series introduced in 1971 (Wikipedia, 2022e).

The generations of computers track the evolutions of semiconductors, from transistors in 1947 to ultra-large-scale integration in 1984. The improvements in semiconductor technology followed an observation made by Gordon Moore in 1965 and updated in 1975. Moore was the founder of Fairchild Semiconductor and later Intel Corporation (Intel); he postulated that the density of integrated circuits would double every two years. Today the observation is known as Moore's law and still holds (Wikipedia, 2022h).

Intel released its first microprocessor in 1971, the Intel 4004. Today, the Intel Core I3, I5, I7, I9, and Xeon processors trace their lineage to the Intel 4004 – conforming to Moore's law.

2.1.2 The development of the internet

Communication over a wire isn't new; for example, the Morse Telegraph used Morse Code (Wikipedia, 2022d) and later the telephone, a voice device. The internet originated with a Defense Advanced Research Projects Agency (DARPA) project to build and connect computer networks that included researchers in the US, France, and the UK (Wikipedia, 2022f). ARPANET was the first network that featured distributed control and wide-area packet switching (Wikipedia, 2022a).

The Department of Defense made TCP/IP, created by a team led by Vint Cerf and Bob Kahn, the standard for all military computer networking in 1982. Three years later, the Internet Advisory Board conducted a workshop for the computer industry promoting TCP/IP, which led to its increased commercial use (History Computer, 2021).

There are a couple of other components of digital evolution worthy of a brief discussion, starting with the World Wide Web (WWW or the web). In 1980, Tim Berners-Lee, while working at CERN, built a personal database called ENQUIRE, which was also a way to play with hypertext (Wikipedia, 2021c). Hypertext is a software approach to linking topics on a computer screen with related information. As used on the web, hypertext is the clickable link you see in a web browser. The term "hypertext" was coined by Ted (Theodor) Nelson as part of his Project Xanadu (Wikipedia, 2022i) – there is a form in use today called HTML, based on Tim Berners-Lee's efforts to adapt Nelson's hypertext.

2.1.3 The rest of the puzzle – digital cameras, cell phones, IoT, cloud computing, and beyond

Steven Sasson invented the self-contained digital camera while working for Kodak in 1975 (Wikipedia, 2021f). The digital camera first appeared in a mobile or cellular phone in 1999 in the Kyocera VP-210 (Android Authority, 2021). The first cell phone was invented by Martin Cooper while working for Motorola in 1973. The first cell phone with internet access was the Nokia 9000 Communicator in 1996 (Pingdom, 2010).

---

6   One of the authors worked on operating systems and compilers during the early phases of his IT career. The increased complexity started with the system architecture and continued through quality assurance (including testing). There was regular testing and evaluation of these products because of the increased complexity of operating systems and language compilers. Besides testing to make sure every change worked as expected and didn't break anything in the product, it was also essential to determine any impact on the application programs that used the compiler or ran on the operating systems.

Another piece of the digital evolution versus digital transformation puzzle exists in the internet of things (IoT) – physical objects that contain sensors, software, and computational capabilities that can connect and exchange data with other devices and systems using communications networks or the internet (Wikipedia, 2022g).

The term "internet of things" was coined by Peter Lewis in 1985. The idea of a "smart device" was discussed circa 1982 at Carnegie Mellon University, while the internet was still ARPANET. A modified Coca-Cola vending machine reported its inventory and temperature. This vending machine was the first non-computer hardware connected to the ARPANET (Wikipedia, 2022g).

Today the IoT applies to consumer applications (e.g., smart homes, smartwatches), medical devices, transportation (e.g., global position system [GPS] tracking, navigation, and electric vehicles[7]), building and home automation, industrial applications, manufacturing, and more.

Cell phones versus supercomputers

We don't think of cell phones as powerful computing devices, provided they do what we want within an acceptably short time. The reality is that our cell phones are extraordinarily powerful computing devices. Consider the following (The Clever, 2017):

- The first supercomputer, released in 1964, was the Control Data Corporation (CDC) 6600, three times faster than its closest competitor. It was capable of 3 million floating-point operations per second (megaflops). The deprecated iPhone 5S, circa 2013, was capable of nearly 77 billion floating-point operations per second (gigaflops) (Wikipedia, 2021b)
- In 1994, the Intel Paragon XP/S 140 benchmarked at a speed of 143 gigaflops (TOP500, n.d.). The 2014 Samsung Galaxy S5 was close, with a speed of 142 gigaflops.

These are just two examples that demonstrate the computing power in our hands and the practical reality of Moore's law.

The tendency is to believe that cloud computing is relatively new; it's not. Cloud computing had its origins in the 1950s (IBM, 2017) when mainframe computers were installed in what today would be called a datacenter, except it was a single massive computer, not racks of computers and related devices. Dumb terminals allowed multiple users to access this central computing resource. In the 1960s, both time-sharing and remote job entry were popular.

We are dependent on our digital devices. As the number of connections grows, so does the related complexity of protecting the interactions between devices.

2.1.4   Digital evolution and digital transformation

We've discussed the development of digital technology from the context of evolution, not transformation. When viewed from the lens of history, there wasn't a specific "transformation" that impacted everyone.

Organizations don't decide to transform. Instead, the organization hits a pivot point – an event (or set of circumstances) that forces a strategic change, for example, the organizations that made significant changes to survive Covid-19. Typically, the events that cause the pivot are less obvious or immediate. However, they involve a similar realization: there is a "survival" reason to stay ahead or play catch-up with the competition.

Technology *enables* the pivot (transformation); it's not a *cause*.

---

7   Electric vehicles (EVs) are mobile computers that look like cars or trucks, dependent on software to control their functionality. Consider that Tesla can provide additional capabilities and updates over the air (OTA) using cellular networks as a software update without the need for a service call. We'll have more to say about this from a security context later in this chapter.

2.2 Evolving threat landscape

Why spend time examining the evolution of the threat landscape? Do we know the current high-risk levels associated with data exfiltration, ransomware, and more? The answer to the question is in this quote from Sun Tzu's The *Art of War*:

> *"If you know the enemy and know yourself, you need not fear the result of a hundred battles. If you know yourself but not the enemy, for every victory gained, you will also suffer a defeat. If you know neither the enemy nor yourself, you will succumb in every battle."*

Make no mistake: it is war – cyberwar!

2.2.1 Brief history of malware

It's probably not a surprise that the history of computer viruses and malware tracks the evolution of digital computing. The seminal academic work in the area was a paper released in 1966, based on a series of lectures in 1949 by mathematician John von Neumann at the University of Illinois (Wikipedia, 2022b) titled "Theory of Self-Reproducing Automata" (von Neumann, 1966). The paper described a design approach to enable a computer program to reproduce itself. This approach to software design described the theoretical basis for the modern computer virus.

The first known attempt to demonstrate the possibilities expressed in von Neumann's paper was the Creeper Virus (Wikipedia, 2022b), written by Bob Thomas at BBN Technologies in 1971 as an experiment to determine the likelihood of a self-replicating program (Exabeam, 2019). Many early computer viruses were designed to answer the question, "Is it possible to …?" Creeper was a worm that replicated itself and spread to Digital Equipment Corporation (DEC) computers connected to the ARPANET. It displayed the message, "I'm the creeper, catch me if you can!" (Exabeam, 2019).

The first internet worm, known as the Morris Worm (FBI, 2018), was created by Robert Morris and released in November 1988 from an MIT-based computer. While the worm did not damage or destroy files, it did cause many vital government and university functions to slow to a crawl because of how it spread. Several organizations had to wipe their systems or disconnect them from the network. The Morris Worm caused damages estimated to be between $100,000 and millions.

> *"The Morris Worm inspired a new generation of hackers and a wave of Internet-driven assaults that continue to plague our digital systems to this day."*
> (FBI, 2018)

Today, the most prevalent attack is ransomware, which encrypts data (and potentially exfiltrates it). Sometimes threat actors do both: they exfiltrate the data, then encrypt it and demand a ransom. Consider the following shortlist (you can find analysis references in the referenced sources – some of the analysis includes cybersecurity controls that might have mitigated or prevented the impact):

- In December 2013, over 11 GB of data was stolen from the retailer Target, including over 40 million credit card numbers and private data on over 70 million customers. The bad actors gained access to Target systems by spoofing a vendor's credentials (SANS Institute, 2014)

- Anthem Health Insurance had the personal information of close to 80 million Americans exposed to hackers (Infosec, 2016; Privacy Risks Advisors, 2017)
- When hackers broke into Home Depot systems, they were undetected for nearly 5 months (SANS Institute, 2015b), and they obtained details of 56 million credit and debit cards and 53 million email addresses
- A nation-state bad actor (assumed to be North Korea) exfiltrated over 12 terabytes of data, over 47,000 unique social security numbers, and more (SANS Institute, 2015a; Risk Based Security, 2014)
- More recently, the SolarWinds breach impacted over 18,000 organizations and was called "the largest and most sophisticated attack the world has ever seen" by Brad Smith, president of Microsoft (Wikipedia, 2021e). Hackers compromised legitimate software updates for the SolarWinds product Orion; this group of hackers worked for the Russian Foreign Intelligence Service and was identified as Cozy Bear. The compromised update became a Trojan horse with a backdoor that communicated via HTTP to third-party servers (Mandiant, 2020; SANS Institute, 2021).

The previous attacks used various ways to gain access to the target victims. A partial list of generic attack types includes (Cisco, n.d.; Netwrix, 2018; OWASP, n.d.):

- **Cross-site scripting (XSS)** Attackers use a third-party site to run scripts on the target. A third-party site is infected with malicious code intended to run on the target servers when a request is made to the third-party site. XSS attacks are sometimes related to SQL injection, described later in this list
- **Denial of service (DoS) and distributed denial of service (DDoS)** Sometimes combined with ransomware to encourage payment. These attacks flood systems with traffic to deliberately overload resources and consume bandwidth
- **Drive-by** Threat actors don't have a specific target; they're looking for any random vulnerability. This attack type gets its name from someone driving through a neighborhood looking for open or unsecured Wi-Fi
- **Identification and authentication failures** Including password (default credentials and dictionary attacks), and not using (or using weak) multifactor authentication
- **Malware (viruses, worms, ransomware, spyware, Trojans, and more)** Types of malicious code. A video from Kaspersky explains some of the differences (Kaspersky, 2016)
- **Man-in-the-middle (MitM)** Occurs when attackers insert themselves into a two-party conversation, typically at unsecured Wi-Fi. A CNBC report demonstrates how this works, and how easy it is for the threat actor to accomplish (CNBC, 2017)
- **Phishing (in various forms)** Sending an email that looks legitimate with a malware payload or link to click. A spear-phishing attack targets specific people or titles
- **SQL injection** The insertion of malicious Structured Query Language (SQL) code that forces the server to send information to an illegitimate recipient
- **Vulnerable, outdated, and misconfigured components** Unpatched components, cybersecurity configuration errors.

There is another type of attack called the *zero-day attack* (CNBC, 2021b). This exploits a discovered but undocumented security weakness. The name "zero-day" refers to the amount of time the good guys have to fix the weakness before the bad actors exploit it. In her book *This Is How They Tell Me the World Ends: The Cyberweapons Arms Race*, Nicole Perlroth details a wealth of information about zero-day attacks and the arms race by governments and bad actors to accumulate as many zero-day attacks as possible (Perlroth, 2021). The intent isn't to always use them: accumulation is part of a cybersecurity arms race.

One of the attacks Perlroth covers in her book is the Stuxnet attack, which combined several different types of attacks to create the first cyber weapon. As reported in her book, once analyzed, it provided information to threat actors regarding how to construct a cyber weapon and the opportunity to repurpose the code to craft new attacks.

The idea of a cybersecurity arms race by both governments and threat actors should be scary. Even without this knowledge, it's critical to understand how these bad actors think. They are agile: they try something; if it doesn't work "here," they try someplace else or another type of attack on the original target. The malicious actors have to be right only once to gain unauthorized access. The good guys have to be right all the time.

Another point about the threat actors is critical: they represent an agile, learning, and adaptive organization. To stay current in the game of leapfrog, the good guys have to match this approach, become more agile and adaptive, and work to become a learning organization in the way discussed by Peter Senge (Senge, 2006).

You may use search engines provided by Google, Microsoft (Bing), or DuckDuckGo. Other search engines (such as Ahmia) target the dark web, which requires a Tor browser or similar tools. You want to hire a cybersecurity expert; hackers similarly look for hacker-for-hire or rent-a-hacker (Perlroth, 2021). As reported by Perlroth, people who used to work for governments now either created their own companies and "cyber-tools" or went freelance – some for good, others not so much.

According to the FBI Internet Crime Complaint Center (IC3), in *Internet Crime Report 2020* (FBI, 2020), the number of top-five reported crime types for 2020 exceeded 513,600[8] – that's more than 1,400 per day just in the US. Think about the magnitude of that: it makes the following comment from one of the authors both a statement of fact and a warning: "It's not a matter of if you'll be attacked, it's only a matter of when." This statement underscores another essential point. The organizational goal should be cyber-resilience, not becoming bulletproof. Every organization must plan for the aftermath of an attack. Consider the following comment one of the authors has made regarding cybersecurity for more than 20 years.

"Security is not a preventative; it's only a delaying tactic. The purpose of security is to keep them out long enough so that when, not if, they break in, whatever you're trying to protect is no longer valuable or sensitive. A burglar alarm does not prevent a thief from attempting a break-in; it just makes it a more challenging task."
David Moskowitz

It's almost impossible to prevent an attack; if you think it can be done, consider CNBC's video report "Why the U.S. Can't Stop Cyber Attacks" (CNBC, 2021a).

We started this section with the comment that the development of malware and related attacks tracked the evolution of computing. Initially, the only targets were large systems. Today anything is a target, and, in some cases, anything can be a vector to more valuable resources.

Consider the Target and Home Depot breaches. In both cases, attackers tunneled through a vendor portal to infect a point-of-sale system. Anyone can be a target.

As technology evolves, so does the variety of attacks. The idea of an *attack surface* refers to any organizational vulnerability, including mobile devices, JavaScript, zero-day (or related hidden or unknown vulnerabilities), supply chain (partners and suppliers), your car,[9] and more. The attack can originate from anywhere: the outer edges of the network, boundaries between networks, in your datacenter or between datacenters, and to or from the cloud. As computational speed increases and the connections between devices (including the cloud and IoT) similarly become more numerous, complexity and elevated organizational risk follow.

---

8   The top five types were (1) various forms of phishing, (2) fraudulent payment or delivery, (3) extortion, (4) personal data breach, (5) identity theft.

9   The modern car (including electric vehicles) is a network on wheels (WIRED, 2015).

2.2.2   Cybersecurity breach statistics[10]

The very beginning of this chapter included the following: "malicious actors concentrate on attacking the weakest link: people."

The Verizon Data Breach Incident Report (DBIR) – which we recommend for two reasons – is an excellent source to learn, less from previous incidents and more from the types of attacks malicious actors use. Second, understanding what happened and was reported provides information to update staff awareness training. The report also indicates the truth of the statement at the start of this section about the malicious focus on people: 86% of breaches involved a human element; 61% involved stolen credentials. Ransomware attacks doubled year-over-year to be the third most common type of breach (Verizon, n.d.).

Don't forget insider threats. Consider this from the DBIR, which raises a chilling possibility (emphasis ours):

---

*"The insider breaches that were maliciously motivated have not shown up in the top three patterns in Healthcare for the past several years. But does this mean they are no longer occurring, **or are they still around, but we just aren't catching them**?"*
(Verizon, n.d.)

Recall that we didn't know about the Snowden leaks until he provided information to the press (Wikipedia, 2022c). There is help for this type of threat at the CERT Insider Threat Center (Carnegie Mellon University, 2017).

There is another type of insider threat that does not have malicious intent. Two examples in the DBIR are privilege abuse and data mishandling. Privilege abuse typically occurs when users have access rights that they don't need to do their job, and use elevated access capability. While some groups might combine data mishandling with privilege abuse, it occurs when someone accesses sensitive information they aren't authorized to access. Data mishandling also occurs when data is improperly handled or protected by someone authorized (for example, taking it home to read, when it shouldn't leave the premises).

2.3   Lessons learned

What can we learn from past breaches?

First, it's essential to pay attention to breaches at other organizations, whether or not they're in your industry sector. If people at Home Depot had followed this recommendation and paid more attention to the Target breach, the impact at Home Depot might have been mitigated or avoided.

The breach at Target resulted from a phishing attack directed at vendors that yielded Target login credentials. The hackers used the purloined credentials to infiltrate Target's systems. They could explore and tunnel from a vendor portal to the point-of-sale (POS) terminals and load a malicious package that exfiltrated customer data.

Target was the focus of an attack because the hackers read a case study about the company on the Microsoft website that documented the use of Microsoft software at Target, including detailed information about Target's infrastructure, including the POS.

---

10   The information in this section is based on Verizon's 2021 Data Breach Investigations Report (Verizon, n.d.).

Target documented compliance with various standards; that was not sufficient. The lesson is to base cybersecurity strategy on risk, not compliance. Use multiple layers of protection – sometimes called *defense-in-depth*. Segregate the network. Why and how does a vendor get access to POS? Use multifactor authentication so that a stolen user ID and password are insufficient to gain access.

The SANS Institute website[11] provides a detailed analysis of the Target breach (SANS Institute, 2014). Why does it make sense to review this (and other breach investigations)? That's part of the point: learn from them, don't dismiss them. If the prevailing attitude is "It can't happen here," then it will happen – it's only a matter of when. The other reason to use these reports is to spark imagination regarding what and how malicious actors think, which might, if you're lucky, suggest a proactive action before an attempted attack.

No one thought about a supply chain attack until the SolarWinds breach. In this case, threat actors weaponized updates to the SolarWinds Orion IT monitoring and management software. The ultimate target for these bad actors was not SolarWinds: it was its customers! One of the lessons is the creativity and patience of the attackers. Another lesson is to look at supply chain trust differently. Consider the application of *zero trust*. Zero trust[12] is an approach to cybersecurity that denies automatic trust to anything or anyone, inside or outside the organization.

The idea of zero trust architecture raises another critical point: there's more to successful attacks than technical attack surfaces. The two others are on equal footing. Failure to consider all three is one way to permit bad actor success. The three attack vectors are *people, practice*, and *technology*.

Previously we covered the idea of resilience versus being bulletproof (i.e., we're fully protected). Resilience is an architecture issue that starts with understanding risk and incorporating it as an essential aspect of organizational strategy.

To be clear, we define architecture as the documentation of the structure of digital assets, their relationships and patterns of interaction, and the environment in which they reside, communicate, and interact.

- **Structure** Identifies the components
- **Relationships** Identify how they are connected
- **Patterns of interaction** Identify how, under what conditions, and with what controls the components communicate
- **Environment** Identifies the physical location and the overall organizational context in which each component fits and is used by or granted access to other components

Note: for this discussion, people and practice are architecture components.

The US National Counterintelligence and Security Center (NCSC) has additional resources based on lessons learned from breaches:

- Protecting Critical and Emerging U.S. Technologies from Foreign Threats (NCSC, 2021)
- National Insider Threat Task Force Mission Fact Sheet (NITTF, n.d.).

Read the documents in a broader context than just national security. Recognize the inherent risk associated with digital assets, which requires senior organizational management to adopt an enterprise risk management approach – a topic covered in more detail in the next chapter.

---

11   SANS stands for "SysAdmin, Audit, Network and Security."
12   There is a NIST publication on zero trust that is worth reading for more information on this subject (Rose *et al.*, 2020).

CHAPTER 3

Cybersecurity and business risk

3 Cybersecurity and business risk

*"A lot of times, people look at risk and ask, 'What are the odds that I will succeed?'
A different way to look at risk is to ask, What's the worst thing that would happen if I failed?'"*
Dave Hitz, founder and Executive Vice President of NetApp

The predominant perception suggests that cybersecurity is (or should be) a technical problem involving a technical response. If there is a breach, it's up to the technical departments to identify, detect, modify, patch, or fix the problem while the business concern addresses the marketplace fallout. Consider the following from Peter Drucker (emphasis added):

*"Asked what a business is, the typical [businessperson] is likely to answer, 'An organization to make a profit.' The typical economist is likely to give the same answer. The answer is not only false, it is [also] irrelevant ... the concept is worse than irrelevant: it does harm ....
There is only one valid definition **of business purpose, to create and retain a customer**."*
(Drucker, 1973)

The point is that the business side rarely looks at the technical side as an active participant in creating and retaining customers. The business side typically views technology as an unavoidable black box of arcane lore – a necessary evil – us (business) versus them (technology).

This approach usually leads organizations to assign responsibility for cybersecurity and associated risk to technology departments. This approach has its basis in the questions the organization asks. Consider the following sample questions typically raised from a technology perspective:

- What is our current cybersecurity investment?
- Will tool "X" solve this issue?
- How much should I spend?
- What is the cost if ...?
- How much do others spend?
- How do we measure (technology) cybersecurity performance?
- What are the most significant threats that we should work to build protection against?
- Are we in compliance ...?

These are the wrong questions. Let's take them apart.

- Questions about cost as strictly a monetary issue miss the holistic issues of reputation, trust, and other intangibles
- Questions about metrics miss a connection to governance
- Questions about protection against threats miss the mark. You don't protect against threats; you protect data and systems appropriately
- Compliance addresses different issues than cybersecurity.

These and other questions address technology departments as if they were outside the business purpose raised by Drucker – to create and retain customers. The questions suggest a bifurcation between business and technology departments, and treat cybersecurity as a potential subject of blame rather than taking a whole-organizational approach.

The real issues need to address people and practice, and technology.[13] The real issues need to address a strategic (i.e., whole-organizational) approach to cybersecurity.

The Executive Summary from the NIST-CSF version 1.1 contains the following:

"Similar to financial and reputational risks, cybersecurity risk affects a company's bottom line. It can drive up costs and affect revenue. It can harm an organization's ability to innovate and to gain and maintain customers. Cybersecurity can be an important and amplifying component of an organization's overall risk management."
(NIST, 2018)

There are two fundamental ways to approach integrating cybersecurity risk into organizational strategy. We recommend a principle-based approach that acknowledges cybersecurity risk as an inherent part of the strategy that we call *strategy-risk* – considered as a single entity.

> **Strategy-risk**
>
> Organizations typically treat strategy and risk separately – possibly consigned to two separate departments. Cybersecurity changes the dynamic. Risk must be an integral part of every strategy, which requires different thinking. Instead of thinking about strategy *and* risk, think about a single entity: strategy-risk.

This approach to strategy-risk supports the idea that digital business value *creation* requires digital business value *protection*. Simply put: any value that is not appropriately protected has no value to the consumer. This link between value creation and value protection is another reason we address strategy-risk as a single entity.

The concepts behind strategy-risk and linking digital value creation with digital value protection may require different thinking. Why? The way we think about a problem or challenge affects the questions we ask to address the problem. Consider the questions above. They originated from a technical perspective. When we apply a different mental model, cybersecurity applied to the whole organization, we must ask other questions.

Instead of technical questions, ask questions that address the business or enterprise level. For example:

- What are the critical business systems?
- What are the underlying IT systems, data, and services that enable, support, or deliver these business services?
- What is the appropriate level of protection for these systems and data to mitigate the business risk?
- Where are the associated data and applications stored for each of these business systems? Does the data have appropriate assured protection? (Assured protection means third-party cloud data protection meets organizational requirements specified in a contract, not assumed)
- What is the risk to the business if any of these systems or data is compromised? (This question also addresses priority – the most risk to the business should get first attention)

---

13   As noted in section 2.3 and reiterated here, the only three things an organization can change or improve are people, practice (or process), and technology.

- Are suppliers or partners involved with the storage, transmission (including transit through), or processing of the associated business data applying appropriate protections?
- How do we know? Are we sure? (Ask these last two questions in response to the answers to the questions above.)

The questions suggest a measured and considered cybersecurity approach that includes strategy-risk and the creation and protection of digital business value. These questions begin by taking a principle-based approach to enterprise risk management. Principles are immutable, apply to the whole organization, and fit the notion of strategy-risk. This approach is part of a different mental model.

3.1   Understanding enterprise risk management

Before covering the COSO principles, we need to look at four general principles[14] applicable to all organizations.

- **Customers drive value** There are three aspects of value: to whom is "this" valuable; identify the appropriate level of protection that includes how the value should be protected; and the maintenance of value as conditions change
- **Change is constant** While this might appear to be an oxymoron, the principle points to the need to make "change" an organizational capability
- **Adopt and apply systems thinking** (This is covered in detail in the companion book, *A Practitioner's Guide to Adapting the NIST Cybersecurity Framework*.) The behaviors within a system are inexorably linked to its structure. The outcomes a system produces equally depend on both structure and behavior
- **Risk is an intrinsic aspect of strategy** This is expressed in two ways: the concept of strategy-risk combined with the focus on decisions that enable and support value creation and protection. [15]

Combining strategy and risk into strategy-risk elevates risk as an essential aspect of strategy that applies to the entire organization. Strategy-risk also helps define a strategic approach to enterprise risk management. This applies on various levels: strategy and governance, governance and execution, and measurement. Figure 3.1 illustrates the relationships.

The relationship between strategy-risk and governance defines and codifies the organizational strategic intent. The relationship between governance and execution/operation delivers appropriately protected value measured by value intent. The right side of Figure 3.1 focuses on goal alignment; the left side focuses on assurance (which may require improvement and realignment) with questions and measurements that uncover and report gaps between expectations and actual – understanding that expectations change because value isn't static.

---

14   These four principles originate with the authors and the DVMS Institute.
15   This two-way expression of risk is also one of the reasons we recommend a principled approach to enterprise risk management using COSO.

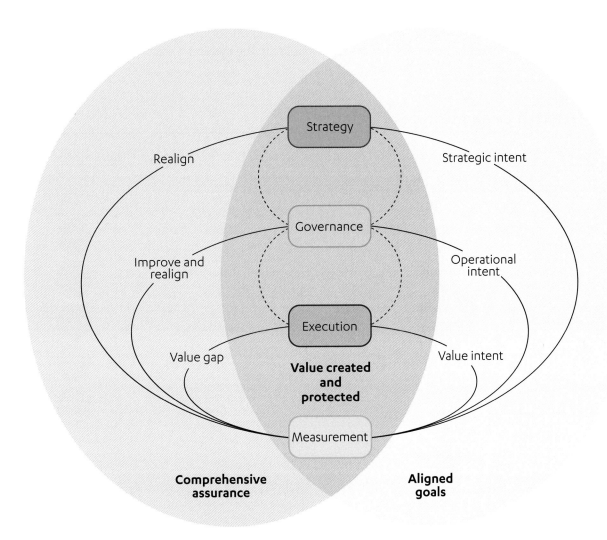

Figure 3.1 Relationship between strategy, governance, execution, and measurement
This figure is a high-level abstraction of the CPD Model discussed in section 3.3

Figure 3.1 also highlights the need for a comprehensive approach to risk: risk management for the enterprise – the whole organization, not individual parts. Also crucial to the selection of an ERM framework is a set of simple principles. Principles facilitate understanding and application. Principles serve as a basis to ask questions: "Does this meet or conform to (the principle)?" This reasoning is also why we recommend the COSO Enterprise Risk Management Framework.[16]

Note: A framework describes what to do; the answer regarding how to do it is left to the organization.

There are 20 COSO principles, divided into five areas:

- Governance and culture
- Strategic and objective-setting
- Performance
- Review and revision
- Information, communication, and reporting.

16   We recommend the Committee of Sponsoring Organizations of the Treadway Commission (COSO) approach. The source for the COSO principles is the COSO Internal Control Integrated Framework (2013) and is used with permission of AICPA. On the COSO website, you can find the executive summary (COSO, 2017) and a summary of the COSO principles and approach (COSO, 2019).

Let's look at each of these individually. Note: In Figures 3.2 to 3.6, a recurring diagram is presented with each group of principles, illustrating where and how the set of principles applies to the whole. The numbered icons in each figure refer to the principle covered in each group.

3.1.1   Governance and culture principles

The principles in this group are foundational to every aspect of enterprise risk management. Governance, informed by strategy-risk, establishes the tone, the approach, the expectations, and the basis for enforcement, and underpins the attention and broad responsibility for cybersecurity.

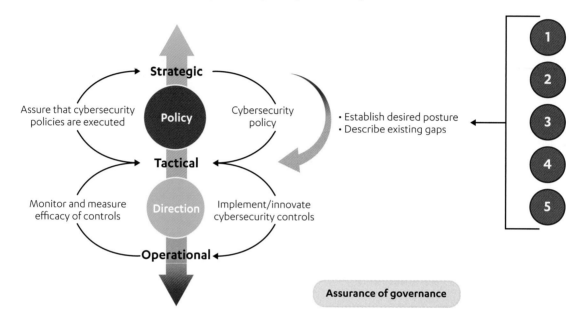

Figure 3.2 Governance and culture principles

The principles in this group are:

1. **Establish board risk oversight** This principle defines the group that has primary responsibility for risk management. The board of directors is responsible for the oversight and governance that supports management's ability to deliver the strategic intent

2. **Establish operating structures** Recall the link, previously noted, between organizational structure and organizational behavior. Establish a structure that supports and enables the desired behaviors

3. **Define the desired culture** This is linked to Principle 2. Culture is the manifestation of organizational behaviors that are linked to organizational structure. Culture can be defined; once defined, it can be achieved (Groysberg *et al.*, 2018)

4. **Demonstrate commitment to core values** The core values must be articulated and communicated, with buy-in by all

5. **Attract, develop, and retain capable individuals** Previously, we discussed the need to consider people and practice in addition to technology. This principle highlights the critical need to consider human resources (people, not a department) as essential resources to achieving business objectives.

3.1.2 Strategy and objective-setting principles

The essence of strategy-risk requires the integration of cyber risk into the development of plans that express the strategic intent within the context of and consistent with organizational (business) objectives. To do this effectively requires the consideration of internal and external risk factors. The principles in this group support the establishment of an organizational risk appetite.

Figure 3.3 Strategy and objective principles

The principles in this group are:

6. **Analyze the business context** This principle requires the organization to consider the potential impact of each business context on the organizational risk profile

7. **Define the risk appetite** Define the risk appetite to support the creation, protection, and delivery of business value

8. **Evaluate alternative strategies** The maintenance of value requires innovation at the strategic level to explore alternatives and their potential impact on the organizational risk profile

9. **Formulate business objectives** The essence of strategy-risk requires the organization to define risk-informed objectives at multiple levels that align with and support the organizational strategic intent.

3.1.3   Performance principles

Performance principles focus on the organization's ability to execute its business objectives. In the same way that we link value creation to value protection, performance links execution with assessment. The organization must identify and assess cyber risks that can impact the achievement of business objectives. This ongoing process requires the organization to monitor performance changes, to develop a portfolio view of the amount of organizational assumed risk.

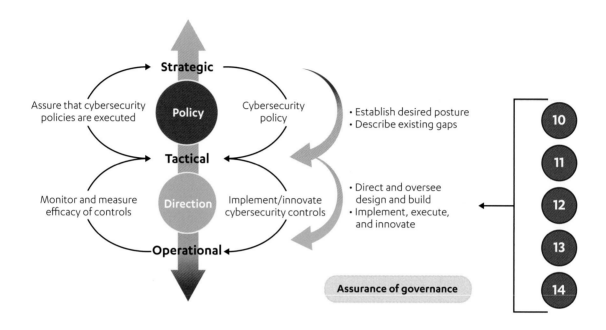

Figure 3.4 Performance principles

The principles in this group are:

10. **Identify risk** Identify risks impacting performance behaviors that affect the delivery of the strategic intent and related business objectives. For example, is it an internal or external risk?

11. **Assess the severity of risk** The assessment of risk begins with the business/enterprise questions introduced in the opening part of this chapter (starting with "What are the critical business systems?")

12. **Prioritizing risk** The same set of questions also helps prioritize the risk response

13. **Implement risk response** Identify and implement an appropriate risk response

14. **Develop a portfolio view** This principle addresses a holistic view of risk. The organization should have a portfolio of products and services it offers (externally and internally). The principle extends the portfolio view to include risk to each product or service.

3.1.4   Review and revision principles

An organization can only sustain value delivery to stakeholders by providing ongoing review and (incremental) improvement at the execution/operation level or (disruptive) innovation at the strategic/governance level.

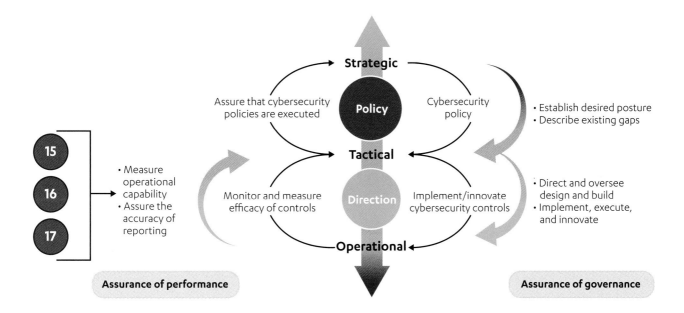

Figure 3.5 Review and revision principles

The principles in this group are:

15. **Assess substantial changes** Projects are the typical mechanism to introduce significant change. Include a risk-based assessment of these changes, which might impact the achievement of business objectives to create and protect digital business value. Ideally, this should occur at the feasibility stage of the project and during the conduct of the project. Waiting until after closing the project is leaving it too late

16. **Review risk and performance** It is essential to provide an ongoing review of organizational performance with full consideration of risk

17. **Pursue improvement in enterprise risk management** The application of ERM is not a "once and done." Conditions continually evolve, which is one of the reasons we suggest that the organization must cultivate and develop "change" as an innate capability.

3.1.5   Information, communication, and reporting principles

Communication occurs when there is an exchange of information or news. The ability to change, revise, and improve depends on continual communication. The practical application of pervasive (i.e., organization-wide) communication facilitates the organizational capability to respond to cyber risks. It is essential to use internal and external sources of information to support this endeavor. Leverage technology to capture, process, manage, and support communication throughout the organization. Communication focuses on all aspects of an organization, including culture, performance, and risk.

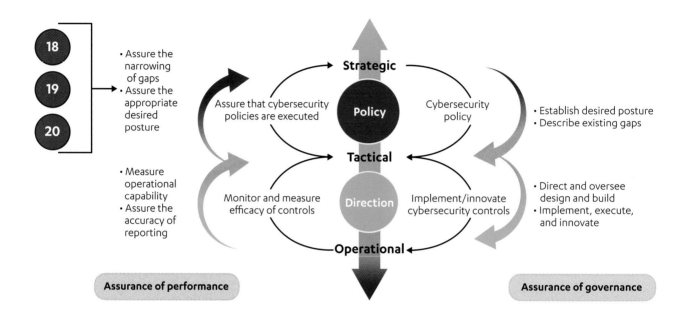

Figure 3.6 Information, communication, and reporting principles

The principles in this group are:

18. **Leverage information and technology** Note the use of the word "leverage." Use technology to scale, to automate, and to decrease the time to identify, detect, and respond to cyber events – approach technology as a tool, not the end

19. **Communicate risk information** Communication is essential to support ERM

20. **Report on risk, culture, and performance** Reporting builds on the monitoring that is part of the performance principles and the improvement in ERM that is part of the review and revision principles. In addition to reporting on risk and performance, reporting also includes information regarding the achievement of the desired culture (see Principle 3).

3.2 ERM is an essential precursor to the adoption of the NIST-CSF

We've discussed risk without defining it, so let's start with some basic definitions (Freund and Jones, 2015).

A *threat* is anything that can cause harm. A *vulnerability* is an exploitable weakness that results in the realization of a threat to achieving business objectives (i.e., impacting the ability to create, protect, and deliver value). A *risk* is the presence of a threat, combined with a vulnerability and the likelihood of occurrence. The *impact* is the effect of the risk if it occurs (i.e., a breach).

What is a risk for the organization? Revisit the questions in the opening part of this chapter (also referenced in section 3.1.3). These questions, and others, support developing answers to this question. With this in mind, we can take the material thus far and see how it aligns with the risk-based approach at the core of the Framework for Improving Critical Infrastructure Cybersecurity, version 1.1 (NIST-CSF) (NIST, 2018).

This section briefly introduces the components of the NIST-CSF (Chapter 4 examines it in detail). It comprises three elements: the Framework Core, the Framework Implementation Tiers, and a Framework Profile.

The Framework Core consists of five nonlinear continuous functions (activities) that we call capabilities: Identify, Protect, Detect, Respond, and Recover. The Implementation Tiers provide a context for the organization to determine the degree to which the organizational cybersecurity risk management practices exhibit the characteristics defined in the NIST-CSF. The Framework Profile represents organizational needs-based outcomes based on applying the Framework categories (practice areas) and subcategories (practices). Profiles express both the current state and the desired state.

3.2.1 Framework Core

The above five capabilities are part of the core. Each activity comprises practice areas (what NIST-CSF calls *categories*) and practices (*subcategories* in the NIST-CSF). Example practice areas or categories include "asset management" and "identity management and access control." Example practices or subcategories include "physical devices and systems within an organization are inventoried" and "remote access is managed."

3.2.2 Framework Tiers

The NIST-CSF defines four Tiers: Partial, Risk-informed, Repeatable, and Adaptive. Each Tier represents increasing attention, rigor, and sophistication to cybersecurity risk management practices. Tiers support the determination of the extent to which business objectives and needs inform cybersecurity risk management. Do not equate Tiers with a maturity model. Use the concept of Tiers to support organizational decisions regarding cybersecurity risk management.

The decision to move from Tier 1 (partial) to Tier 2 and beyond should be based on an evaluation of feasibility, including a cost-benefit analysis that supports a cost-effective reduction of cybersecurity risk. The issue should not address how much to spend, without considering the future return on the investment in the form of reduced cybersecurity risk and exposure.

Chapter 4 covers the Framework Tiers in detail. Their names are:

- Tier 1: Partial
- Tier 2: Risk-informed
- Tier 3: Repeatable
- Tier 4: Adaptive.

3.2.3   Framework Profile

Framework Profiles characterize the alignment of the Framework Core (capabilities, practice areas, and practices) with the strategic intent inclusive of business objectives and needs, risk tolerance, and resources. The purpose of the Framework Profile is to enable the organization to determine a roadmap to reduce cybersecurity risk in alignment with organizational goals.

Establishing the current ("as-is" or "now") Profile surfaces what the organization is currently doing. Creating a target Profile defines the future outcomes needed to achieve the desired business-driven cybersecurity risk management goals. A gap analysis provides the way to achieve the target Profile.

3.2.4   How a principled approach to ERM supports the adoption of the NIST-CSF

When the COSO principles are adopted, this provides the organization with a starting point for adopting the NIST-CSF.[17] The principles address whole-organizational issues that support a business-first approach to cybersecurity. Recall the five groups of principles introduced in section 3.1:

- Governance and culture
- Strategic and objective-setting
- Performance
- Review and revision
- Information, communication, and reporting.

The principles included in the governance and culture group are consistent with the NIST-CSF description of the core capabilities (functions), which suggests they need to become an aspect of a dynamic operational culture to address the continually changing aspects of cybersecurity risk. There is a similar alignment with the other groups of COSO principles.

---

17   The NIST-CSF is not directly implementable. Each NIST-CSF practice (subcategory) maps to cybersecurity informative references that define the rules and requirements of each set of cybersecurity controls. Treat the informative reference description of a control as requirements for the control. The context of these requirements is to apply the appropriate amount of care and detail to each cybersecurity control necessary and sufficient to fit the organizational need; this idea is expanded in more detail in the companion volumes, *A Practitioner's Guide to Adapting the NIST Cybersecurity Framework* and *A Business Guide to Living on the Edge of Chaos*.

3.3   Introducing the CPD Model

We've already introduced a high-level abstraction of the CPD Model in Figure 3.1 (CPD being an abbreviation for creating, protecting, and delivering digital business value). The complete model appears in Figure 3.7. This section covers the basics of the model; there's more detail in the companion volume, *A Practitioner's Guide to Adapting the NIST Cybersecurity Framework*.

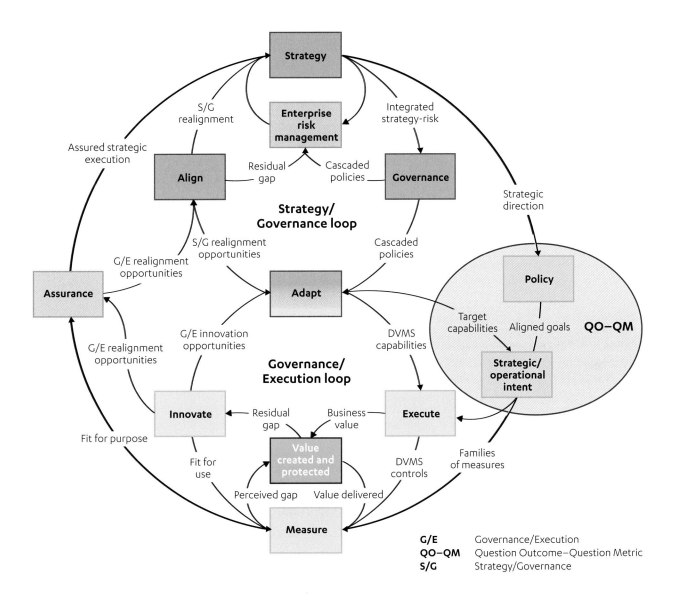

Figure 3.7 The CPD Model

A crucial element to understanding the CPD Model is to see the whole – presented as a system,[18] more specifically a system of systems. The thinking required is similar to considering your car as a transportation system comprising a fuel system, a steering system, a braking system, and more. While you can examine the "sub-systems" in detail, your ultimate objective is to use the car to get from point A to point B. You address the component systems when and as needed to handle a particular challenge to preserve the overall purpose of the car as a transportation system.

---

18   There is a chapter on systems thinking in the companion volume *A Practitioner's Guide to Adapting the NIST Cybersecurity Framework*.

Abbreviations

The following are introduced here and covered in more detail in Chapter 5.

- **CPD** Create, protect, and deliver (digital business value)
- **QO–QM** Question Outcome–Question Metric
- **SG loop** The Strategy/Governance loop in Figure 3.7
- **GE loop** The Governance/Execution loop in Figure 3.7.

The CPD Model represents a dynamic model of systems to create, protect, and deliver digital business value. The fundamental principle behind the model is that the business value created must be protected at a level proportional to its value to the organization.

The two outer arcs represent the flow of strategy and governance (on the right, through QO–QM) and assurance (on the left). Governance stems from developing a strategy composed of five aspects: *plan, ploy, pattern, position,* and *perspective* (Expert Program Management, 2018). For our purposes, we'll focus on the aspect of strategy that develops a plan – a plan to achieve long-term goals that acknowledge varying degrees of uncertainty. The outer governance loop establishes the strategy.[19] The assurance loop monitors, measures, and reports opportunities to sustain the delivery of protected value as conditions change; it also provides confidence that everything is within expected or allowed tolerances.

There are two inner loops. The top loop (SG) addresses strategy and governance; the bottom one (GE) addresses governance and operation (execution). The SG loop establishes the desired scope and rigor for cybersecurity initiatives at the organization. It considers the organizational Tiers and determines the current and target Profiles. The GE loop executes the policies to create, protect, and deliver digital business value.

Notice that technology does not appear in Figure 3.7; this is intentional. Technology is a tool, not an end – it supports each loop presented in the CPD Model. The CPD Model represents a different level, a different type of thinking, essential for the organization to succeed in its cybersecurity initiatives.

Everything in the CPD Model is connected, which requires the consideration of the whole, not just a particular part or department of the enterprise (in other words, a different type of thinking, a view through the right end of the telescope). Consider the following questions:

- How does what we do (or are planning to do) in the GE loop impact the SG loop?
- What is the impact of the SG loop on the GE loop?
- Have we paid appropriate consideration to both the creation and the protection of digital business value?
- The model also addresses the assurance-related questions, "How do you know?" and "Are you sure?"

Each of the four loops in the CPD Model applies to the whole organization, for either planning or execution/operation. The model fits any organization, which does not mean that every organization applies every aspect of it. Every organization uses parts of the model; as it grows and matures, it uses more of the model with more applied rigor. The critical idea regarding the model is that it applies to the whole organization. Thinking about cybersecurity as a technology-first initiative isn't part of the model.

Applying the model to the entire organization is essential to treating value creation and value protection as different sides of the same coin – another reason to elevate cybersecurity responsibility to the board of directors (or similar governing body).

---

19   QO–QM is our variation of GQM+Strategies® that is covered in *A Practitioner's Guide to Adapting the NIST Cybersecurity Framework* (Basili *et al.*, 2014).

Take a step back for a moment. W. Edwards Deming, Peter Drucker, and many others have written about quality. Consider these two quotes from Deming's *Out of the Crisis* (Deming, 2000):

"Why is it that productivity increases as quality improves? Less rework."

"Low quality means high costs. Defects are not free.
Somebody makes them and gets paid for making them."

And this from Drucker's 1999 edition of *Management Challenges for the 21st Century* (Drucker, 1999):

"What is value to the customer is always something quite different from what is value or quality to the supplier. This applies as much to a business as to a university or hospital."

There are two things of note. Deming documents the link between quality and cost, which echoes the comment from NIST in the Executive Summary of the Framework. Second is Drucker's link between value and quality (quoted in Chapter 1 and repeated here).

"Customers pay for what is of use to them and gives them value.
Nothing else constitutes 'quality.'"
(Drucker, 1985)

The CPD Model takes a total system view of strategy-risk, governance, execution/operation, and assurance. It represents a way for the organization to create and protect digital business value.

Building on the idea of a relationship between quality and value, we suggest a relationship between quality and cybersecurity. Low quality, or lack of attention to cybersecurity at the board of directors level, increases costs. Refer to the quotation from the Executive Summary in the NIST-CSF earlier in this chapter: "cybersecurity risk affects a company's bottom line" by driving up costs. One way to look at the CPD Model is to understand that it addresses quality and cybersecurity. Value that is not appropriately protected has little to no value to the intended stakeholders who link value and quality; if the quality doesn't meet expectations, the perception of value diminishes. Unprotected value is an aspect of low quality.

The idea of strategy-risk is an integral part of the model, and is a driver behind combining the creation with the protection and delivery of digital business value. If it makes it easier to think differently about cybersecurity as an organizational responsibility rather than a technical one, then think of cybersecurity initiatives as a property of what the organization does to achieve a desired level of quality.

Introduction to the NIST-CSF

4 Introduction to the NIST-CSF

> *"Having been involved in cybersecurity for almost thirty years and observing the continuing devastation and disruptions from an ever-increasing number of cyber-attacks on the public and private sectors, it was time to pursue a new direction in cyber defense and return to some fundamental, time-tested concepts and principles for protecting our systems and networks."*
> Dr. Ronald Ross, NIST Fellow

The National Institute of Standards and Technology (NIST) produced the Framework for Improving Critical Infrastructure Cybersecurity[20] in response to Presidential Executive Order (EO) 13636 (Improving Critical Infrastructure Cybersecurity, February 2013); the executive order represented a reaction to events in 2012.

By the end of that year, the Department of Homeland Security analysts "had responded to 198 attacks on US critical infrastructure systems – a 52 percent increase from the previous year" (Perlroth, 2021). The President signed the EO in February 2013; the first version of the Framework was released a year later. While the EO represented a reactive response to events, it directed an increased proactive stance for critical infrastructure.

Also that year, the US Congress passed the Cybersecurity Enhancement Act of 2014. This Act codified the EO into law and directed NIST to create a cost-effective and efficient approach to cyber risk management that allowed adopting organizations to prioritize risk with a performance-based approach. Although it is directed at organizations comprising critical national infrastructure, it has broader applicability. The Cybersecurity Act of 2015 promoted the public and private sharing of cybersecurity information. The current version (1.1) was released in April 2018 and will evolve as needed.

Figure 4.1 illustrates how the Framework has evolved since 2013.

> *"The Framework focuses on using business drivers to guide cybersecurity activities and considering cybersecurity risks as part of the organization's risk management processes. The Framework consists of three parts: the Framework Core, the Implementation Tiers, and the Framework Profiles."*
> (NIST, 2018)

---

20   The Framework does not describe specific cybersecurity controls. Appendix A of the Framework provides links to specific cybersecurity informative references (e.g., COBIT 5, ISO/IEC 2700, NIST Special Publication 800-53).

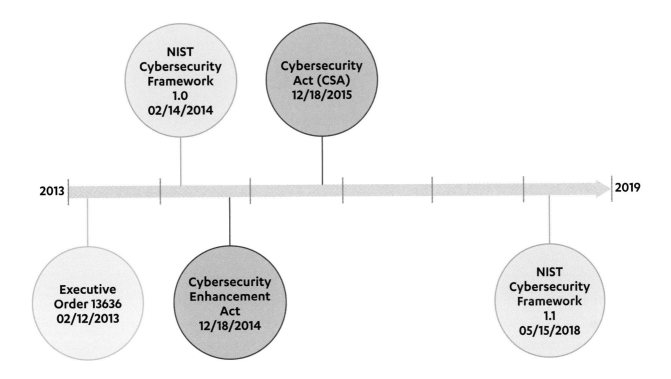

Figure 4.1 Framework timeline

The Framework describes the "what and why" required to manage cybersecurity risks; it describes the essential capabilities an organization must have to take a risk-based approach to managing cybersecurity risks. It also explains why the capabilities are crucial. The Framework stresses the unique nature of organizational risks, priorities, and digital assets. It assumes that the tools and methods used to achieve the outcomes vary at any specific organization.

The Framework is technologically neutral. It references existing standards, guidelines, and practices that evolved with technology to provide global applicability. This approach enables using existing and emerging standards, and promotes market competition; it also supports faster diffusion of new cybersecurity technologies.

> **Cybersecurity Enhancement Act of 2014**
>
> "To provide for an ongoing, voluntary, public-private partnership to improve cybersecurity, and to strengthen cybersecurity research and development, workforce development and education, and public awareness and preparedness, and for other purposes."
>
> "Support the development of a voluntary, consensus-based, industry-led set of standards, guidelines, best practices, methodologies, procedures, and processes to cost-effectively reduce cyber risks to critical infrastructure."

Another aspect of the Framework is that it provides a common taxonomy to (NIST, 2018):

- Describe a current cybersecurity state
- Describe a future cybersecurity state
- Identify and prioritize opportunities for improvement within the context of continual and repeatable processes
- Assess progress toward the target future state
- Communicate risk to stakeholders (internal and external).

> **Understanding terminology**
>
> The Framework uses a specific set of terms in describing the Framework Core: *functions, categories*, and *subcategories*. Many readers may find it easier to relate to them in more familiar terms used in other frameworks:
>
> - **Functions** Are a set of high-level activity groups representing the strategic view of the lifecycle for cybersecurity risk management. Other frameworks describe these as *capabilities* – each providing the power or ability to do something.
> - **Categories** In the Framework, categories subdivide functions into groups of cybersecurity outcomes. Other frameworks typically describe these as *practice areas*, aggregating the outcomes of one or more related practices.
> - **Subcategories** Represent the level that describes specific outcomes. Most people would recognize these as *practices*.
>
> The **informative references** provide the specific cybersecurity control requirements.

The Framework is not a "one-size-fits-all" approach to managing cyber risks. However, it applies to all public, private, and military organizations. How can this be? The answer is: It's a framework, not a cookbook, in the sense that it is not directly implementable. It describes a way for any organization to improve its approach to cybersecurity risk.

In the following sections, we'll dive deeper into the Framework to understand its Core, Tiers, and Profiles, linking implementation to Tiers introduced briefly in the previous chapter. We'll also cover how it supports self-assessment.

One important note: While the purpose of the Framework was to address challenges in critical US infrastructure, its use also extends to organizations that were not part of the specific target sectors, both inside and outside the US.

4.1   Framework Core

The Framework Core provides four components that enable an organization to achieve cybersecurity outcomes specific to its desired cybersecurity posture:

- Functions
- Categories
- Subcategories
- Informative references.

The Framework takes a risk-based approach, focusing on outcomes. When adapting the Framework guidance to its context,[21] the adopting organization has the flexibility to tailor those outcomes to meet its unique needs. Consider the following sentence taken from the Executive Summary of the Framework:

"The Framework focuses on using business drivers to guide cybersecurity activities and considering cybersecurity risks as part of the organization's risk management processes."
(NIST, 2018)

4.1.1   Functions

The Framework uses functions to provide a basic set of high-level activities to *identify* and *protect* digital assets, *detect* cybersecurity events, respond to these events, and *recover* as necessary. These functions provide the structure and guidance required for an organization to:

- Manage cybersecurity risk
- Make risk management decisions
- Respond to a dynamic threat landscape
- Continually establish a heuristics-based approach to improving organizational capabilities.

The five functions of the Framework Core (NIST, 2018) are:

- **Identify** Develop an organizational understanding necessary to manage cybersecurity risk to systems, people, assets, data, and capabilities

  - The activities in the Identify function are foundational for *effective use of the Framework*
  - Understanding the *business context, the resources that support critical functions, and the related cybersecurity risks* enables an organization to focus and prioritize its efforts, consistent with its *risk management strategy and business needs*

- **Protect** Develop and implement appropriate safeguards to ensure delivery of critical services

  - The Protect function supports limiting or containing *the impact* of a potential cybersecurity event

- **Detect** Develop and implement appropriate activities to identify the occurrence of a cybersecurity event

  - The Detect function enables the timely discovery of cybersecurity events

- **Respond** Develop and implement appropriate activities to respond to a detected cybersecurity incident

  - The Respond function supports the ability to *contain the impact* of a potential cybersecurity incident

- **Recover** Develop and implement appropriate activities to maintain *resilience plans and restore any impaired capabilities or services* from a cybersecurity incident

  - The Recover function supports *timely recovery to normal operations to reduce the impact* of a cybersecurity incident.

---

21   It's important to note that the Framework does not present the requirements for cybersecurity controls. Instead, it provides a mapping from subcategories (practices) to various cybersecurity informative references for specific control requirements.

4.1.2   Categories

Categories represent the high-level objectives of the functions; categories aggregate related subcategory outcomes. One way to think about categories is to relate them to practice areas – these group similar practices and their outcomes relative to a specific organizational capability.

Table 4.1 Functions and categories

Function	Framework category	Question
Identify	Asset management	What digital assets need protection?
	Business environment	
	Governance	
	Risk assessment	
	Risk management strategy	
	Supply chain	
Protect	Access control	What safeguards are available?
	Awareness and training	
	Data security	
	Information protection, processes, and procedures	
	Maintenance	
	Protective technology	
Detect	Anomalies and events	What techniques can help identify incidents?
	Continuous cybersecurity monitoring	
	Detection processes	
Respond	Response planning	What techniques can limit the impact of an incident?
	Communications	
	Analysis	
	Mitigation	
	Improvements	
Recover	Recovery planning	What techniques provide resilience?
	Improvements	
	Communications	

> *"Categories are the subdivisions of a Function into groups of cybersecurity outcomes closely tied to programmatic needs and particular activities."*
> (NIST, 2018)

4.1.3 Subcategories

> *"Subcategories further divide a Category into specific outcomes of technical and/or management activities. They provide a set of results that, while not exhaustive, help support achievement of the outcomes in each Category."*
> (NIST, 2018)

Subcategories are similar to practices, where the associated processes and activities produce specific outcomes. A practice area is a collection of related practices that produce a specific organizational outcome.

4.1.4 Informative references

> *"Informative References are specific sections of standards, guidelines, and practices common among critical infrastructure sectors that illustrate a method to achieve the outcomes associated with each Subcategory. The Informative References presented in the Framework Core are illustrative and not exhaustive."*
> (NIST, 2018)

The informative references listed in the Framework mapping provide specific outcomes for cybersecurity control requirements. They describe the control, what it seeks to achieve, and its intended outcome. An organization that adopts the Framework needs to adapt the functions, categories, and subcategories to its specific context. The Framework recognizes the potential need for the adopting organization to use guidance from additional sources (including new or revised standards, guidelines, or practices) and other informative references.

Figure 4.2 illustrates the relationships between functions, categories, subcategories, and informative references.

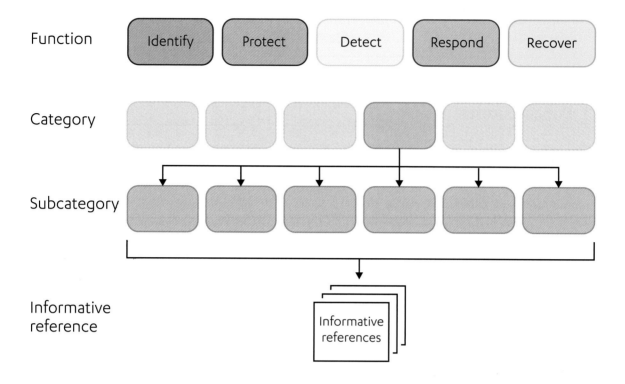

Figure 4.2 Functions, categories, subcategories, and informative references

4.2 Implementation Tiers

> *"The Framework Implementation Tiers ('Tiers') provide context on how an organization views cybersecurity risk and the processes in place to manage that risk."*
> (NIST, 2018)

Implementation Tiers enable an organization to determine its current risk management capabilities and describe its desired future state capabilities. The difference represents the gap the organization must close to achieve its desired state. Tier selection considers the internal organizational needs, external requirements, and threat landscape.

> *"Tiers are meant to support organizational decision making about how to manage cybersecurity risk, as well as which dimensions of the organization are higher priority and could receive additional resources."*
> (NIST, 2018)

However, Tiers should not be confused with maturity models. Tiers describe the organizational rigor demonstrated in the three aspects of risk management.

"Successful implementation of the Framework [by adapting one or more cybersecurity informative references] is based upon achieving the outcomes described in the organization's Target Profile(s) and not upon Tier determination."
(NIST, 2018)

Figure 4.3 shows how the four Implementation Tiers relate to the risk management process, the integrated risk management program, and external participation. The following sections describe the characteristics of each Implementation Tier with respect to the three attributes.

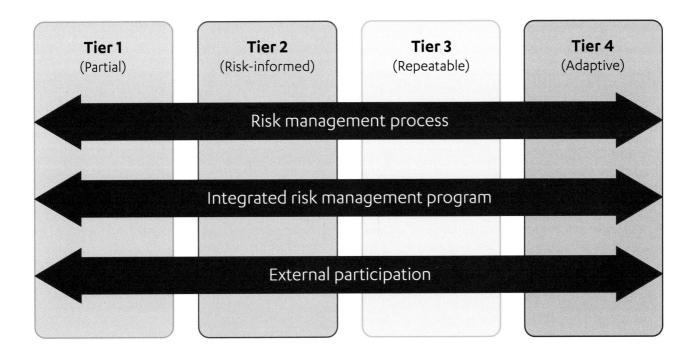

Figure 4.3 Implementation Tiers

4.2.1 Tier 1: Partial

- **Risk management process** Organizational cybersecurity risk management practices are informal; risk management is ad hoc and sometimes reactive. Prioritization of cybersecurity activities is typically not based on organizational risk objectives, the threat environment, or business/mission requirements

- **Integrated risk management program** There is limited organizational awareness of cybersecurity risk. The implementation of cybersecurity risk management is irregular and incident-based due to varied experience or information gained from outside sources. The organization may not have processes that enable sharing of cybersecurity information

- **External participation** The organization does not understand its role in the larger ecosystem concerning its dependencies or dependents. The organization does not collaborate with, or receive information (e.g., threat intelligence, best practices, technologies) from, other entities (e.g., buyers, suppliers, dependencies, dependents, Information Sharing and Analysis Organizations [ISAOs] [CISA, n.d.], researchers, governments), nor does it share information. The organization is generally unaware of the cyber supply chain risks of the products and services it provides and uses.

4.2.2   Tier 2: Risk-informed

- **Risk management process** While management may approve risk management practices, these practices are not always incorporated into any organization-wide policy. Organizational risk objectives, the threat environment, or business requirements inform the prioritization of cybersecurity-related activities and protections

- **Integrated risk management program** The organization is aware of cybersecurity risk, but a formal organization-wide approach to managing cybersecurity risk is lacking. There is informal sharing of cybersecurity information within the organization. Consideration of cybersecurity in organizational objectives and programs may occur at some but not all levels of the organization. Cyber risk assessment of organizational and external assets occurs, but is not typically repeatable or reoccurring

- **External participation** Generally, the organization understands its role in the larger ecosystem concerning its dependencies *or* dependents, not both. The organization collaborates with and receives information from other entities, and generates some of its information but does not always share it. Additionally, the organization is aware of the cyber supply chain risks associated with the products and services it provides and uses, but does not act proactively on those risks.

4.2.3   Tier 3: Repeatable

- **Risk management process** Organizational risk management practices are formally approved and expressed as policy. The organization regularly updates its cybersecurity practices by applying risk management processes to adapt to changes in business/mission requirements and a changing threat and technology landscape

- **Integrated risk management program** Cybersecurity risk management exists throughout the organization. Based on organizational risk, policies, processes, and procedures are defined, implemented, reviewed, and assessed. Methods are in place to respond consistently and effectively to changes in risk. Staff possess the knowledge and skills to perform their assigned roles and responsibilities. The organization consistently and accurately monitors the cybersecurity risk of organizational assets. Senior executives, both cybersecurity and non-cybersecurity, communicate regularly regarding cybersecurity risk. Senior executives ensure consideration of cybersecurity through all lines of operation in the organization

- **External participation** The organization understands its role, dependencies, and dependents in the larger ecosystem and may contribute to the broader community understanding of risks. It regularly collaborates with other entities, receives information from them (which complements internally generated information), and shares information with them. The organization is aware of the cyber supply chain risks associated with the products and services it uses and provides. Additionally, it usually acts formally upon those risks, including written agreements to communicate baseline requirements, governance structures (e.g., risk councils), and policy implementation and monitoring.

4.2.4 Tier 4: Adaptive

- **Risk management process** The organization adapts its cybersecurity practices based on previous and current cybersecurity activities, including lessons learned and predictive indicators. Through continual improvement incorporating advanced cybersecurity technologies and practices, the organization actively adapts to a changing threat and technology landscape and responds in a timely and effective manner to evolving, sophisticated threats

- **Integrated risk management program** An organization-wide approach to managing cybersecurity risk uses risk-informed policies, processes, and procedures to address potential cybersecurity events. When it is making decisions, the relationship between cybersecurity risk and organizational objectives is clearly understood and considered. Senior executives monitor cybersecurity risk in the same context as financial risk and other organizational risks. The organizational budget is based on understanding the current and predicted risk environment and risk tolerance. Business units implement the executive vision and analyze system-level risks in the context of established organizational risk tolerances. Cybersecurity risk management is part of the organizational culture, and evolves from an awareness of previous activities and continuous awareness of activities on the organization's systems and networks. The organization can quickly and efficiently account for changes in business/mission objectives in approaching and communicating risk

- **External participation** The organization understands its role, dependencies, and dependents in the larger ecosystem and contributes to the broader community understanding of risks. It continuously receives, generates, and reviews prioritized information used to analyze its risks as the landscape of threats and technology evolves. The organization shares that information internally and externally with other collaborators. The organization uses real-time or near real-time data to understand and consistently act upon cyber supply chain risks associated with the products and services it provides and uses. Additionally, it communicates proactively, using formal (e.g., agreements) and informal mechanisms to develop and maintain strong supply chain relationships.

4.3 Framework Profiles

> *"The Framework Profile ('Profile') is the alignment of the Functions, Categories, and Subcategories with the business requirements, risk tolerance, and resources of the organization."*
> (NIST, 2018)

An organization establishes a Profile based on the Framework to determine the current state of any specific cybersecurity activity. A Profile documents this state by assessing demonstrable outcomes of function, category, and subcategory alignment – the organization examines its cybersecurity capabilities, practice areas, and practice outcomes. This evaluation uses the cybersecurity control requirement outcomes enumerated in the selected informative reference as the point of comparison. The assessment of the current state describes where you are.

Similarly, the organization uses Profiles to describe the desired state (set of outcomes). This target or future state helps the organization to identify and analyze the gaps in its capabilities, practices, processes, and activities, and develop a roadmap to close them. Using a risk-based approach, the organization considers its internal needs, external requirements (legal, regulatory, compliance, etc.), and threat landscape. The Framework encourages the organization to participate in cyber risk management with other organizations with similar needs, requirements, and threat landscapes. The information used to establish a Profile is shown in Figure 4.4.

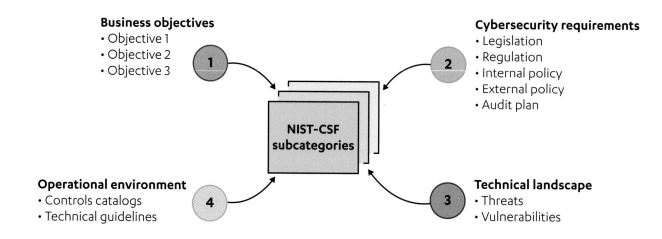

Figure 4.4 Framework Profile inputs

4.3.1 Getting there

An essential aspect of Framework Profiles is that they represent how the organization currently supports its business/mission goals. Use Framework Profiles to communicate with organizations, the supply chain, and stakeholders by describing the gap between the current and desired states of cybersecurity risk management combined with the necessary time, money, and resources to close the gap. Later in this chapter, we'll discuss how the Framework supports self-assessment and continual improvement programs.

> *"The Framework provides a common language to communicate requirements among interdependent stakeholders responsible for the delivery of essential critical infrastructure products and services."*
> (NIST, 2018)

For example, the adopting organization may create a target Profile for internal use, or to communicate to an external service provider or an organization in its supply chain. Framework Profiles also have applicability during due diligence in an acquisition. This is not just for organizations that form part of the critical infrastructure segment: any organization might benefit from Framework Profiles.[22] Because the Framework is descriptive, not prescriptive, organizations are free to tailor Profiles specific to their business/mission context.

Framework Profiles provide demonstrable evidence about how well the organization protects the digital business value it creates. This idea underscores the need to treat cybersecurity in a broader context than IT; it is a "whole business" problem, *not* an IT problem.

---

22 While the NIST was tasked with addressing the US national critical infrastructure, the Framework can be applied/used by any organization in any country.

4.4 Create or improve a cybersecurity program

When an organization makes the strategic decision to adopt the Framework, it is rarely a greenfield situation. The organization typically already has cybersecurity capabilities, practices, processes, and activities. An assessment establishes the current baseline. The differences between the current and desired states define the gap. The adopting organization must adapt the necessary control requirements to meet its internal needs, external requirements, and threat landscape. The gaps determine whether the organization must create new capabilities or improve existing ones.

4.4.1 Coordination of Framework implementation

The Framework's approach to coordinating the implementation or improvement of the organization's cybersecurity risk management is straightforward, and is illustrated in Figure 4.5.

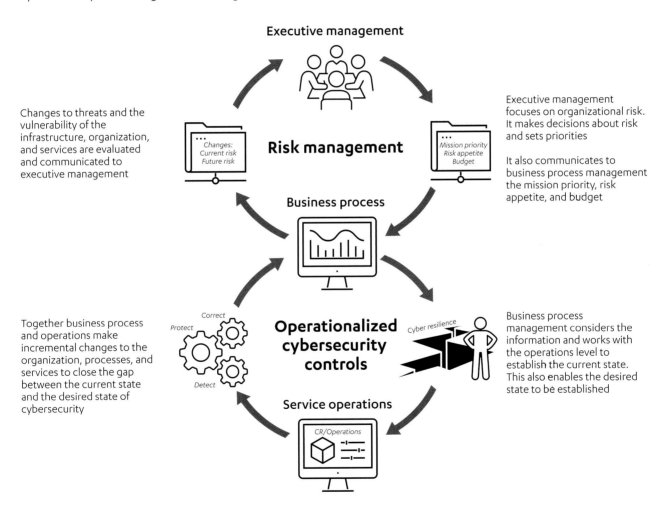

Figure 4.5 Coordinating the implementation or improvement of cybersecurity capabilities

"The executive level communicates the mission priorities, available resources, and overall risk tolerance to the business/process level. The business/process level uses the information as inputs into the risk management process and then collaborates with the implementation/operations level to communicate business needs and create a Profile. The implementation/operations level communicates the Profile implementation progress to the business/process level. The business/ process level uses this information to perform an impact assessment. Business/process level management reports the outcomes of that impact assessment to the executive level to inform the organization's overall risk management process and the implementation/operations level for awareness of business impact."

(NIST, 2018)

4.4.2   Establishing a cybersecurity program

The Framework uses a standard seven-step approach (NIST, 2018) to create or improve organizational cybersecurity capabilities, as shown in Figure 4.6. Repeat the steps as necessary to achieve the desired organizational cybersecurity state:

- **Step 1: Prioritize and scope** The organization identifies its business/mission objectives and high-level organizational priorities. With this information, it makes strategic decisions regarding cybersecurity implementations, and determines the scope of systems and assets that support the selected business line or process. The Framework is adaptable to support the different business lines or processes within an organization, which may have different business needs and associated risk tolerance. A target Implementation Tier reflects the associated risk tolerances.

- **Step 2: Orient** Once the scope of the cybersecurity program is determined, the organization identifies related systems and assets, regulatory requirements, and overall risk approach. The organization then consults sources to identify threats and vulnerabilities applicable to those systems and assets.

- **Step 3: Create a current Profile** The organization develops a current Profile by assessing and documenting the specific category and subcategory outcomes from the Framework Core. Note any partially achieved outcomes to support subsequent steps by providing baseline information.

- **Step 4: Conduct a risk assessment** Base this assessment on the overall organizational risk management process or previous risk assessment activities. The organization analyzes the operational environment to determine the likelihood of a cybersecurity event and the impact that it could have on the organization. Organizations must identify emerging risks, and use cyber threat information from internal and external sources to understand the likelihood and impact of cybersecurity events.

- **Step 5: Create a target Profile** Create a target Profile that focuses on assessing the Framework categories and subcategories that describe the desired organizational cybersecurity outcomes. The organization may develop additional categories and subcategories to account for unique organizational risks. It may also consider the influences and requirements of external stakeholders such as sector entities, customers, and business partners when creating a target Profile. The target Profile should appropriately reflect criteria within the target Implementation Tier.

- **Step 6: Determine, analyze, and prioritize gaps** The organization compares the current and target Profiles to determine gaps. Next, it creates a prioritized action plan to address gaps, reflecting the mission drivers, costs and benefits, and risks to achieve the outcomes in the target Profile. The organization then determines the resources necessary to address the gaps, including funding and workforce. Using Profiles in this manner encourages the organization to make informed decisions about cybersecurity activities, supports risk management, and enables it to perform cost-effective, targeted improvements.

- **Step 7: Implement action plan** The organization determines which actions to take to address the gaps identified in the previous step, and then adjusts its cybersecurity practices to achieve the target Profile. For further guidance, the Framework identifies example informative references regarding the categories and subcategories, but the organization should determine which standards, guidelines, and practices, including those that are sector-specific, work best for its needs.

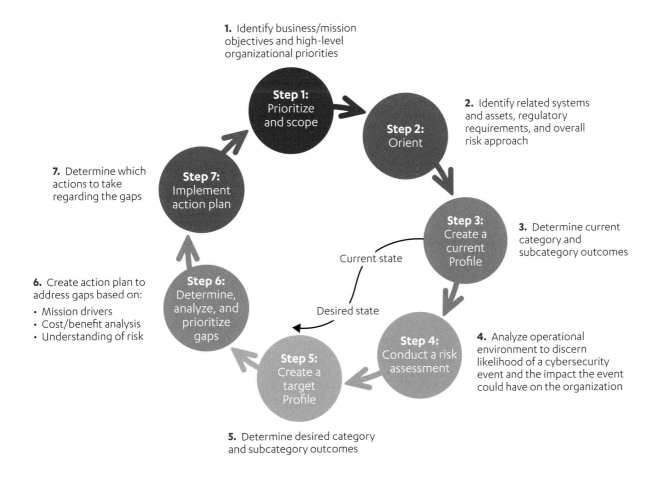

Figure 4.6 The NIST-CSF uses seven steps to establish or improve a cybersecurity program

4.4.3 Cybersecurity risk self-assessment

To be effective, an organization must have a clear and comprehensive understanding of the relationship between its organizational objectives and the cybersecurity capabilities that support those outcomes. The Framework describes how an organization links the value it creates to its capabilities to protect that value. The previous chapter discussed the CPD Model and how value creation and protection are inextricably linked. The model uses strategy-risk to describe strategic and operational intent combined with the measures and metrics necessary to determine whether the practices create, protect, and deliver business value that is fit for use and fit for purpose. It enables the instrumentation of organizational systems to fit two perspectives: the implementor of the system and the auditor of system performance. It supports the organization in identifying demonstrable artifacts that enable it to assess its cybersecurity state continually.

Self-assessment enables an organization to (NIST, 2018):

- Evaluate the organizational approach to cybersecurity risk management by determining current Implementation Tiers
- Make choices about how different portions of the cybersecurity execution should influence the selection of target Implementation Tiers
- Prioritize cybersecurity outcomes by developing target Profiles
- Determine the degree to which specific cybersecurity steps achieve desired cybersecurity outcomes by assessing current Profiles
- Measure the degree of implementation for controls catalogs or technical guidance listed as informative references.

The adopting organization assures that the execution of strategic policies is effective and efficient through continual self-assessment. It establishes its risk tolerances and continually monitors its performance. This capability also enables the organization to evaluate its risk appetite as its internal needs, external requirements, and dynamic threat landscape change.

As the organization works to close cybersecurity gaps in a dynamic environment, it develops the ability to make faster and better decisions about its risk posture and protect the business value created. This approach is essential in today's interconnected business ecosystems – an organization is only as secure as the weakest link in its supply chain. The organization can share meaningful risk information up and down the supply chain to forge and maintain trusted cybersecurity relationships.

It's important to understand that an organization's cybersecurity tolerances will change over time as its needs, requirements, and threat landscape change. Based on the measures and metrics used to assess its strategic and operational intent performance, the organization is assured that its cybersecurity tolerances will continually adapt to its current context.

CHAPTER 5

Introduction to NIST-CSF and the CPD Model

5 Introduction to NIST-CSF and the CPD Model

Let's start with why we created a model to support creating, protecting, and delivering digital business value. The Framework guidance informs the adopting organization about what is essential and why. It provides a structured approach to achieve the desired cybersecurity capabilities. However, a framework is not implementable: the organization can adopt it; adoption requires governance decisions.

Once the decisions and policies are in place, the NIST-CSF supports the organizational effort to adapt the guidance to meet organizational needs, including the external requirements and the threat landscape.

5.1 The "first principles" of the CPD Model

The CPD Model represents a mental model used to realize the Framework guidance – in other words, how to think about the organizational capabilities needed to operationalize the Framework by implementing the cybersecurity controls of the selected informative references.

Four fundamental principles underpin the CPD Model:

- Customers drive value
- Change is constant
- Adopt and apply systems thinking
- Risk is an intrinsic aspect of strategy.

5.1.1 Customers drive value

There are three aspects of value described in this model:

- Value requires a point of view (to whom is this valuable?)
- Protect digital business value at a level proportional to its value to the organization
- Protecting value is not once and done – maintain it or lose it.

Value is subjective, so the point of view defines to whom "this" is valuable. All value has one or more stakeholders. The CPD Model subsumes stakeholders and their point of view as part of strategic and operational intent. This idea is covered in depth in the Question Outcome–Question Metric (QO–QM) section (see section 5.2.7).

Value must be protected. Value that is not protected has no value. In the context of cybersecurity, unprotected value faces unlimited and unmitigated risks. The organization assumes the consequences when an unprotected asset that supposedly provides value is stolen or made inaccessible.

Protecting value is not once and done – maintain it or lose it. Value exists in a dynamic environment and is subject to changes to internal needs, external requirements, and a dynamic threat landscape.

An organization adopting the Framework and using the CPD Model must seek clarity and focus on what matters when creating, protecting, and delivering digital business value. The CPD Model ensures the organization can identify and close performance gaps.

5.1.2   Change is constant

Change happens all the time. An organization's internal needs change, its external requirements change, and the threat landscape is equally dynamic. The seemingly contradictory phrase "change is constant" also becomes a principle. The CPD Model represents a dynamic system that accommodates the changing organizational needs, requirements, and threat landscape.

The CPD Model enables an organization to continually adapt to its context by identifying gaps caused by change and seeking to close them. Fundamentally, the organization approaches everything as an opportunity to innovate. No matter what it is, the current state represents the starting point to pursue continual innovation to close gaps between the current and desired states.

"Change is constant" means that change is occurring continuously, while "change is a constant" means that change is an always-to-be-expected condition.

To successfully adopt the Framework, the organization *must* make the ability to change a core-mission-critical organizational capability. The CPD Model handles this as a practical matter because it treats any gap as an opportunity to innovate.

5.1.3   Adopt and apply systems thinking

Before we address systems thinking, let's start by answering the question "What is a system?"

A system is a group of interrelated and interacting parts organized to accomplish a purpose. In simple terms, a system is a "whole" that consists of parts with the following characteristics:[23]

- Each part affects the behavior or properties of the whole
- Each part of the system, when it acts within or impacts the system, is dependent on the effect of some other part
- No part of a system (or collection of parts) has an independent effect
- A system is *not the sum of its parts* – it is the *product of interactions* between the parts.

Usually, a complex system is composed of a set of systems or a system of systems. Think about a car. It is a transportation system consisting of a fuel system, a braking system, a transmission system, a sensor system (also a system of systems), and more.

Treat the interactions within a system as behaviors. These behaviors within a system create signals (messages) to other parts of the system or other systems (including external systems). These behaviors occur within a structure: the structure of the system. The idea of behaviors within a structure links these two concepts such that you cannot change one without impacting the other. System behavior and system structure are different sides of the same coin.

Once we understand the idea of a system, we can address the idea of systems thinking as a way to think differently, as developing a different perspective to approach the concept of problem-solving. Typically, we try to analyze parts of the system (for example, root cause analysis (Wikipedia, 2021d)) instead of considering the whole. This approach often leads to "fixes" that expose additional issues, errors, or vulnerabilities.

The CPD Model addresses a different form of thinking about problems because the model is outcome-based. The behaviors of the system components produce its outcomes. In addition, the CPD Model includes consideration for the latency between cause (behaviors) and the observation or detection of the related effect.

---

23   One of the authors audited a course delivered by Dr. Russell Ackoff. This information is based on notes taken during one of his lectures.

This principle is also related to "change is a constant" because all systems will trend toward disorganization (i.e., entropy). The CPD Model considers everything as a candidate for improvement, and will continually adapt to its current context to remain effective at delivering the desired outcomes.

"Structure is the network of relationships that creates behavior. The essence of structure is not in the things themselves but in the relationships of things. By its very nature, structure is difficult to see. As opposed to the events and patterns, which are the usually more observable, much of what we think of as structure is often hidden. We can witness traffic accidents, for example, but it's harder to observe the underlying structure that causes them."
Richard Karash, independent consultant

5.1.4   Risk is an intrinsic aspect of strategy

The CPD Model treats risk as an intrinsic aspect of strategy. An organization *must* adopt an enterprise risk management framework to ensure the business strategy is risk-informed. The CPD Model posits that strategy includes an understanding of the elements of risk. The model presents this idea as *strategy-risk*. Like with "space-time," the two parts of strategy-risk exist together, and one cannot exist separately from the other.

In the same way that no plan is perfect, no strategy is, either: every strategy includes uncertainty and some risk aspect. The CPD Model incorporates the concept of *risk-informed strategy* (strategy-risk) to form strategic policies that seek to mitigate cyber risk through guidance that creates business value and protects it proportionally.

In practical terms, the business objectives that fall out of strategic and management policies result in building protection for the value from the beginning, instead of figuring out how to bolt it on after the fact.

For the business, this approach (to strategy-risk) changes the dynamics associated with cybersecurity. The CPD Model combines value creation and value protection into a single requirement to deliver the expected value for stakeholders. This model eliminates the idea that cybersecurity is a cost center or something to add later (in the development cycle: in effect, bolt on).

5.2   NIST-CSF and the CPD Model

The Framework addresses the "what and why" of cybersecurity capabilities. The CPD Model acts as an overlaid archetype for the adopting organization, thereby providing the roadmap to bring the Framework to "life."

5.2.1   The CPD Model – a system of systems

A system is the product of the interacting behaviors of its component elements. The CPD Model represents a system of systems that aggregate behaviors that create, protect, and deliver digital business value. There can be latency, in any system, between an action and the observation of the results of that action. The CPD Model illustrates this point directly (as shown in Figure 3.7). An organization must be cautious when it seeks to close a performance gap. It is essential to understand the desired outcomes with consideration of the entirety of the CPD Model to ensure changes affect only the desired behaviors and do not create unintended consequences.[24]

---

24   To make any behavioral changes "sticky," it may be essential to change the structure within which the behaviors occur.

The five loops of the CPD Model are:

- Governance/Assurance
- Strategy-risk
- Strategy/Governance
- Governance/Execution
- Value delivered.

5.2.2   Governance/Assurance

The discussion of the CPD Model starts with the overarching concepts of *governance* and *assurance*. Governance is about overseeing the control and direction of the organization. Assurance is being confident of the efficiency and effectiveness of the control and direction.

An organizational strategy is a general plan to achieve one or more long-term goals under conditions of uncertainty. Its strategy can be considered an organizational adaptation of behavior and structure that serves (or appears to serve) an essential function in achieving an evolutionary end. That is a long-winded way to say that it addresses how an organization plans to adapt to its environment to survive and thrive.

In the Governance/Assurance loop of the CPD Model, strategy establishes the overall organizational strategic direction. Governance addresses how the organization makes decisions based on its strategic intent, exerts control internally, and positions itself externally to differentiate itself relative to all others in its market or competitive space. Governance is how an organization makes policies into actionable and measurable business objectives.

Measure the execution of policies through business objectives against the organizational strategic and operational intent. The establishment of performance measures enables the organization to determine whether its policies deliver the expected business value and established capabilities that are fit for use and purpose.

Assurance establishes confidence in executing the strategic policies and achieving their intended objectives. Inherent in this model is that the measures and metrics needed for assurance are designed into the organizational capabilities to create, protect, and deliver digital business value.

5.2.3   Strategy-risk

The strategy-risk loop describes how an organization produces risk-informed strategies by adopting an enterprise risk management framework to formulate a risk-aware business strategy.

COSO has an established set of internal controls that support its enterprise risk management framework. This excerpt from its guidance on internal controls is fundamental to the concept of the CPD Model.

"Each enterprise risk management component includes principles that apply to creating, preserving, and realizing value in an organization regardless of size, type, or location. The principles and their components do not represent isolated, stand-alone concepts. Each highlights the importance of integrating enterprise risk management and the role of decision-making. The Framework outlines considerations to integrate culture, practices, and capabilities into each principle [and] into the entity. These considerations are not exhaustive, but they do demonstrate the range of inputs into decision-making and the exercise of judgment by personnel, management, and the board."
(COSO, 2013)

The organization must evaluate strategy in the context of the risks inherent in each strategy. The CPD Model expresses this relationship through weaving risk into the business strategy so that "the principles apply to creating, preserving, and realizing value." The model represents this approach as "strategy-risk."

5.2.4 Strategy/Governance

The Strategy/Governance loop, illustrated in Figure 5.1, represents the senior leadership's formulation of its business strategy, and promulgates strategic policies that cascade through the management team for execution. The model integrates feedback to realign strategy and policies.

5.2.4.1 Strategy

The organization formulates strategies to modify its essential behaviors or structures to adapt to its dynamic environment. Strategy becomes "risk-informed" by integrating an enterprise risk management framework. The result, "strategy-risk," is used throughout the CPD Model. The Strategy/Governance loop of the CPD Model sets the overall organizational strategic direction.

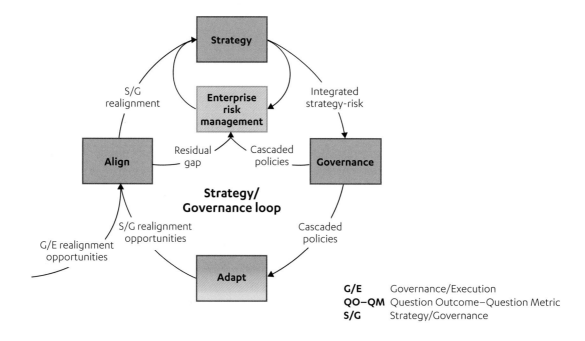

Figure 5.1 Strategy/Governance loop

5.2.4.2 Governance

Governance provides the direction and control over the organizational structures and behaviors in creating and executing policies derived from strategy-risk policies. These policies include guidance on the business objectives, including creating, protecting, and delivering digital business value.

5.2.4.3 Adapt

Strategic policies are adapted by management and subsequently implemented by the Governance/Execution loop (covered in section 5.2.5). This provides feedback to improve the Digital Value Management System (DVMS), innovate opportunities, and strategy and policy realignment.

The DVMS represents a three-layered system covered in more detail in the companion book *A Practitioner's Guide to Adapting the NIST Cybersecurity Framework*. The DVMS is an overlay to the existing capabilities of any organization. The idea of an overlay is essential – it's not a one-size-fits-all; it is a systems model applicable to all, regardless of size. It overlays what the organization does and provides a roadmap for improvement.

5.2.4.4 Align

Alignment requires an assessment of opportunities for policy and strategy from the Strategy/Governance loop and the Governance/Execution loop, and those generated by an overall gap in the execution of strategic policy. It provides input to ERM and assesses realignment opportunities as an input to strategy.

5.2.5 Governance/Execution

The Governance/Execution loop, illustrated in Figure 5.2, addresses strategic policies that cascade into management policies. This cascade guides the development and innovation of DVMS capabilities and the business objectives that drive the creation and protection of digital business value. This loop is responsible for delivering and improving value.

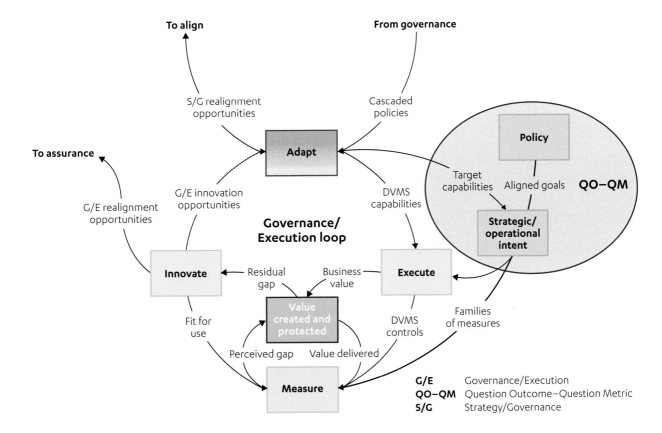

Figure 5.2 The Governance/Execution loop

5.2.5.1   Adapt

Strategic policies are adapted to the organizational need to create, protect, and deliver digital business value. Adaptation is the nexus between Strategy and Execution: management makes strategy-risk policies actionable. It's integral to both the implementation and innovation of the DVMS capabilities and digital business value. It also provides feedback for the realignment of strategic policies and strategies.

5.2.5.2   Execute

The DVMS operates on business objectives to create, protect, and deliver digital business value, and has five core capabilities (Plan, Design, Change, Execute, and Innovate) that are part of the overall systems that form the CPD Model.

5.2.5.3   Measure

The DVMS capabilities and the creation, protection, and delivery of digital business value performance are measured against the strategic and operational intent. Any performance gaps generate feedback as inputs to improve performance. The feedback may also provide insights into policy and strategy realignment.

5.2.5.4   Innovate

The Innovate capability operates on the DVMS capabilities, practice areas, practices, and digital business value. In the CPD Model, innovation plays an integral role in identifying, assessing, and closing gaps in the performance of the DVMS and the delivery of digital business value. Operational performance is assessed against the measures and metrics established by the expressed strategic and operational intent. Innovation opportunities include gaps in digital business value, DVMS performance, and the execution of strategic policies.

5.2.6   Value delivered

One of the "first principles" of the CPD Model is that all digital business value created must be protected at a level proportional to its organizational value. All business objectives that flow from strategy-risk through strategic and management policies embody this principle. Digital business value and its protection are inextricably linked. The principle requires integrating cybersecurity requirements with DVMS capabilities, practice areas, practices, and aggregated processes. Performance gaps reflect changes to conditions regardless of where they originate (internal, external, or the threat landscape).

QO–QM is a method (described in section 5.2.7) of aligning strategic outcomes and developing measures and metrics to assess the delivered digital business value against the expressed strategic and operational intent. Performance gaps are assessed to determine innovation opportunities in delivering digital business value (shortfall between expected and observed), DVMS capabilities in delivering digital business value (shortfall in the capability to deliver as expected), or the execution of strategic policies.

All performance is measured against the schema created by the measures and metrics of the expressed strategic and operational intent. The CPD Model is dynamic, resulting in an ever-changing measurement schema and the DVMS capability to identify, assess, and close performance gaps.

5.2.7 Question Outcome–Question Metric (QO–QM)

Unique to the CPD Model is the Question Outcome–Question Metric (QO–QM) approach to ensure strategic goals align with strategic direction. QO–QM is a modification of the GQM⁺Strategies approach (Basili *et al.*, 2014). QO–QM focuses on aligning strategic goals and the subsequent decomposition of those goals using standard GQM[25] to understand the measures and metrics needed to assure the delivery of digital business value and ensure that the execution of strategic policies is fit for use and purpose.

Strategic direction, expressed as strategy-risk, is used to develop strategic and management policies. The strategic policies identify and align strategic outcomes. These aligned outcomes and the expression of target capabilities become input to the QM portion of QO–QM to develop the measures and metrics used to describe strategic and operational intent.

These measures and metrics are used to create a schema to produce assurance reports that describe any gaps in perceived value delivered, DVMS performance, and the execution of strategic policies.

Innovation in the Governance/Execution loop identifies opportunities to innovate the value created and protected. Assurance identifies innovation opportunities in strategic policies and provides input to the Strategy/Governance loop for policy realignment or strategy for strategic realignment.

QO–QM aligns strategic outcomes, and develops measures and metrics to assess digital business value delivered against the expressed strategic and operational intent. Performance gaps are assessed to determine Innovate opportunities in delivering digital business value (shortfall between expected and observed), DVMS capabilities in delivering digital business value (shortfall in the capability to deliver as expected), or the execution of strategic policies. The CPD Model continually seeks to minimize gaps in strategy-risk, policies, DVMS, and digital business value creation, protection, and delivery.

All performance is measured against the schema created by the measurement and metrics of the expressed strategic and operational intent. The CPD Model is dynamic, resulting in an ever-changing measurement schema and the DVMS capability to identify, assess, and close performance gaps. At the macro level, the Governance/Assurance loop promulgates strategic policies that establish controls to achieve the organizational strategic direction; it also assesses performance to assure the strategic policies are effectively executed. In this model, the strategic direction includes the first principle, that all digital business value created must be protected at a level proportional to its expressed business value.

5.3 Cybersecurity and the CPD Model

Cybersecurity is an inherent aspect of the CPD Model, encapsulated in the concept of strategy-risk.

5.3.1 CPD Model and innovation

Most organizations and frameworks treat the idea of "getting better at something" as *improving*. The CPD Model takes a broader approach, focusing on innovation that subsumes the idea of improvement.

---

25   GQM (goal, question, metric) is an established approach to software metrics to improve and measure software quality. The measurement model has three levels: conceptual (goal), operational (question), and quantitative (metric).

5.3.1.1 Innovation

The NIST Framework provides a seven-step process that describes implementing and improving organizational cybersecurity capabilities. The CPD Model takes a slightly different approach by treating any performance gap (the difference between the current state and the desired state) as an opportunity to innovate.

There are four aspects to innovation:

- Incremental
- Sustaining
- Adaptive
- Disruptive.

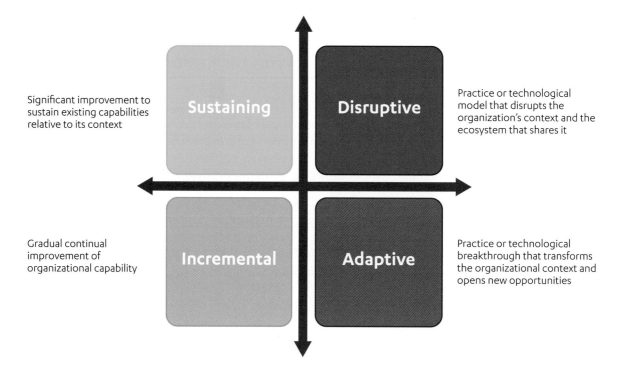

Figure 5.3 Aspects of innovation

Incremental innovation applies when the organization takes continual improvement steps. Each step builds on the progress of the previous steps. This approach is the most common aspect of innovation; it applies to the incremental improvement of business and technical processes or technological capabilities. Improving an existing feature in a software product in a series of successive sprints is one example of incremental innovation. The Framework seven-step model is representative of this approach.

Sustaining innovation addresses more significant steps an organization takes to improve capabilities. This approach is characterized in the seven-step model to implement new functionality, for example, the addition of two-factor authentication.

Adaptive innovation occurs when the organization changes either a practice or a particular use of technology to achieve a new organizational capability that opens new opportunities. An example of this type of innovation occurred when Amazon developed the logistic capacity to shift its small package deliveries to its fleet.

Disruptive innovation occurs when the organization makes a change to a practice or introduces a breakthrough technological advance that disrupts the context of the organization and all who share that ecosystem. Probably one of the most disruptive examples of this occurred when Apple introduced the iPhone. That event acted like an extinction event for many industries that provided products that eventually migrated to the iPhone and later Android platforms.

Why is this important? The Framework assumes that adopting organizations are at some unknown starting point in their cybersecurity capabilities. A seven-step process is suitable for implementing new or improved cybersecurity capabilities. The CPD Model operationalizes the NIST seven-step process, and enables the organization to continually improve and sustain its cybersecurity capabilities and support innovation as either an adaptive change to policy or a disruptive shift in strategy.

5.3.1.2　You are here

To innovate, the organization must have the capability to assess its current state and describe the desired future state of cybersecurity. The difference between these two states represents the gap the organization must close. The last step is to "implement the action plan." As far as the guidance goes, that is the equivalent of saying "magic happens here."

5.3.1.3　The CPD Model operationalizes the seven-step process

Chapter 4 covered the NIST seven steps to establish and improve a cybersecurity program as a generic approach. Here we take a more practical approach and link the NIST approach with the CPD Model.

- **Step 1: Prioritize and scope**　The organization identifies its business/mission objectives and high-level organizational priorities, with risk tolerances expressed in a target Implementation Tier.

  The Strategy/Governance loop of the CPD Model (see Figure 5.1) operationalizes identifying business/mission objectives and high-level organizational priorities. The organization expresses its business objectives in the form of strategic direction and integrated strategy-risk policies. Those policies are inclusive of current and future state risk tolerances

- **Step 2: Orient**　The organization identifies related systems and assets, regulatory requirements, and overall risk approach, and then consults sources to identify threats and vulnerabilities applicable to those systems and assets.

  The CPD Model's strategy-risk policies drive the identification of related systems and assets, regulatory requirements, and the overall risk approach. Enterprise risk management provides the relevant cyber risk input to develop the overall strategic direction and strategy-risk policies. The identification of threats and vulnerabilities occurs within the Governance/Innovation loop, guided by the strategy-risk policies

- **Step 3: Create a current Profile**　The organization develops its current Profile by documenting which category and subcategory outcomes from the Framework Core exist at the organization.

  The assessment of the current organizational state enables the organization to establish the current Framework Profile. This baseline assessment is the starting point for the organization to innovate incrementally or seek new capabilities to sustain within its context. Note that the "current Profile" describes outcomes that are verifiable and quantitative

- **Step 4: Conduct a risk assessment**　This assessment is guided by the overall risk management process or previous risk assessment activities.

  The CPD Model applies the risk assessment of the target Profile by using either previous risk assessments or updated risk assessments that consider changes to internal organizational needs, external requirements, or the threat landscape. The CPD Model embodies two feedback loops that enable the organization to realign strategies or policies, or to improve or sustain cybersecurity operational capabilities. Risk assessment of a desired future state must consider strategic risks and operational aspects when planning a way forward to a desired future state

- **Step 5: Create a target Profile** The organization creates a target Profile that focuses on assessing the Framework categories and subcategories that describe the desired organizational cybersecurity outcomes.

  The CPD Model supports the activities necessary to Plan, Design, Change, Execute, and Innovate to achieve the target state (see Figure 5.2). In doing so, it considers all dependencies on, or interactions with, existing capabilities

- **Step 6: Determine, analyze, and prioritize gaps** The organization compares the current and target Profiles to determine gaps. Next, it creates a prioritized action plan to address gaps that reflects mission drivers, costs and benefits, and risks to achieve the outcomes in the target Profile.

  In the CPD Model, this step occurs in the Governance/Execution loop. The detailed planning and design consider the scope of change to any dependent organizational capabilities and the necessary modifications to close the cybersecurity performance gaps. In addition, planning and design include the instrumentation of the modified capabilities to gather appropriate metrics to ensure they are fit for use and purpose

- **Step 7: Implement action plan** The organization determines which actions to take to address the gaps identified in the previous step, and then adjusts its current cybersecurity practices to achieve the target Profile consistent with the requirements of the selected cybersecurity informative references.

  The CPD Model operationalizes this step through the change, execution, and innovation that adapts the organizational capabilities associated with change. The Governance/Execution loop adapts the new capabilities that have been identified, planned, designed, and built. Execution addresses the operation of the underlying organizational and cybersecurity capabilities to create, protect, and deliver digital business value.

5.3.2   Good to great with nonlinear improvement

The CPD Model supports nonlinear improvement. It supports explicitly incremental and sustaining operational-level improvements to DVMS capabilities (small scale). It also supports potentially adaptive and disruptive changes through the realignment of policies and strategies (large scale).

All innovations result in the dynamic update of the strategic and operational intent, measures and metrics, and the schema used to assess performance gaps (people, practice, and technology). The CPD Model provides multiple feedback paths to support nonlinear thinking and problem-solving, which can be something of a scary concept for organizations that exhibit "less agile" problem-solving.

5.3.3   Critical thinking and nonlinear thinking

> *"Nonlinear thought increases possible outcomes by not being so certain about the starting point for any logic process. Nonlinear thinkers tend to jump forward, and from side to side through the steps of a project, in an effort to see the big picture and tackle those areas where they have the most interest."*
> (McCumber, 2009)

Nonlinear improvement doesn't have to be "messy." The rigor within the CPD Model constrains and focuses on innovation. Its constraints are dynamic, depending on the scope and impact of the innovation. A broader scope and higher impact necessitate more comprehensive constraints initially, but quickly bring solutions into focus. The types of innovation that have nonlinear scope and impact on an organization are shown in Figure 5.4.

The CPD Model can be scaled: that is one of its strengths. It supports applying the Framework's seven-step process in any organization, large or small. It just works.

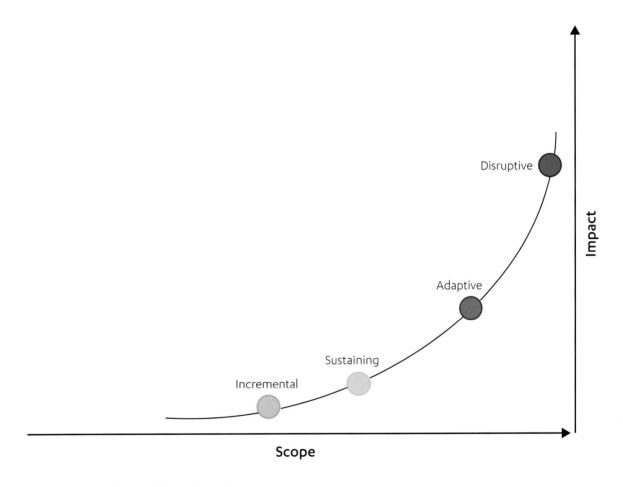

Figure 5.4 Innovation and nonlinear improvement

5.3.4   Working *on* and *in* the CPD Model

Frameworks describe what an adopting organization should think about and why it's essential. A framework is descriptive because it leaves the "what to do" and "how to do it" to the adopting organization to figure out. The CPD Model describes a systems approach for an organization to adapt the Framework guidance to its environmental context.

The organizational adaptation of the Framework guidance is realized in two parts. The first part is implementing or improving the current organizational cybersecurity capabilities to achieve the desired cybersecurity posture. The second part is the execution and improvement of the "new normal" or updated state of cybersecurity capabilities.

The adopting and adapting organization must differentiate between working *on* the system and working *in* the system.

Working *on* the system describes what an adapting organization does to create or improve its cybersecurity capabilities, including people, practice, and technology. It includes the points of view of the implementor and auditor. This dual viewpoint is a critical aspect of the CPD Model because both perspectives are necessary for the planning, design, change, execution, and innovation of the capability to create, protect, and deliver digital business value. The combined perspectives enable the adapting organization to instrument the systems so that both the implementor and auditor can determine whether the new or changed systems deliver the expected business value, meaning the changes are fit for purpose and fit for use.

Working *in* a system is what the adapting organization does to operate the systems that realize the desired organizational cybersecurity capabilities. It also explains how the organization utilizes the data collected from the system to make informed decisions about the system's ongoing fitness for purpose and to identify potential innovation opportunities.

5.3.5   Assessment and closing the gap

The DVMS operationalizes the CPD Model. It represents the minimum set of organizational capabilities necessary for an organization to create digital business value, protect it at a level commensurate to its value, and deliver the desired digital business value to its stakeholders. An adopting organization uses the DVMS as an overlay on top of its existing systems to assess the gap between its current and desired states, including underlying systems supporting the cybersecurity capabilities.

5.3.5.1   CPD adapts the DVMS principles

The CPD Model adapts the four principles[26] of the DVMS:

- **Customers drive value** There are three aspects of value:

  - It requires a point of view (to whom is it valuable)
  - Value must be protected at the appropriate level to the organization
  - The perception of value is dynamic

    The organization must engage with stakeholders to ensure the value delivered matches the value expected; any discrepancy represents an opportunity to innovate (adaptive/incremental or a disruptive/paradigm-shift)

- **Change is constant** The organization must have the core capability to change because everything is subject to change. The CPD Model assumes internal and external needs, combined with the dynamics of an evolving threat landscape, drive change

- **Adopt and apply systems thinking** The behaviors and structures within a system are inextricably linked; there may be latency between cause (behaviors) and the observable related event. All systems tend toward disorganization and therefore must be continually improved to adapt to the organizational environment

- **Risk is an intrinsic aspect of strategy** In the CPD Model, *strategy-risk* is a concept that subsumes the decisions to create and protect digital business value.

---

26   These are the same generic principles initially introduced in Chapter 3.

5.3.6　DVMS core capabilities

The following sections describe each DVMS core capability, along with its practice areas, practices, and outcomes. Processes (intentionally omitted from this book, as they are left to the organization) implement and execute the activities necessary to produce the outcomes. The description includes any internal DVMS relationships, a maturity capability model, and demonstrable artifacts for each outcome at each capability level.

Five core organizational capabilities comprise the Z-X Model (part of the DVMS), as shown in Figure 5.5:

● Plan
● Design
● Change
● Execute
● Innovate.

Each capability has one or more practice areas that aggregate the practices to achieve a minimum organizational capability. The Z-X Model is an aspect of the DVMS Model (covered in more detail in subsequent volumes in this series).

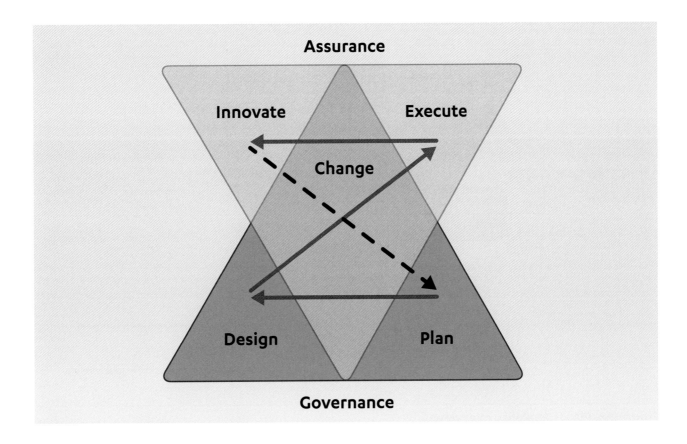

Figure 5.5　Z-X Model of DVMS capabilities

5.3.6.1 Plan

The Plan capability enables the organization to govern, assure performance, create, execute a risk-informed business strategy, manage its portfolio of programs, risks, and projects, and manage the organizational knowledge. The practice areas of the Plan capability subsequently enable the organization to create, protect, and deliver digital business value.

The purpose of the Plan capability subsumes two goals: the creation and delivery of digital business value, and protecting the value delivered at a level proportional with its value to the business.

Five practice areas comprise the Plan capability (see Figure 5.6):[27]

- Governance
- Assurance
- Risk management
- Portfolio, program, and project management
- Knowledge management.

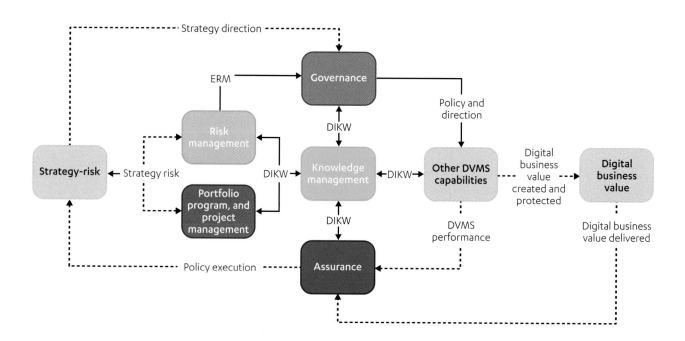

DIKW Data, information, knowledge, wisdom

Figure 5.6 Plan: Capability overview

---

27 In Figures 5.6 to 5.10, *DIKW* stands for Data, Information, Knowledge, and Wisdom. *Data* is raw, potentially nothing more than a stream of numbers. Apply one or more transforms to the data and you get *information* (what and why). Add additional transforms combined with insight and experience, and you get *knowledge* (how). Do this enough, learn from mistakes, learn what works and what doesn't, and you get *wisdom* (why).

5.3.6.2 Design

The Design capability enables the organization to create a straightforward, cohesive approach to creating, protecting, and delivering digital business value. It seeks to develop designs through the system architecture and configuration management practice areas that enable the organization to deliver digital business value and protect it.

Practice areas (see Figure 5.7):

● System architecture
● Configuration management.

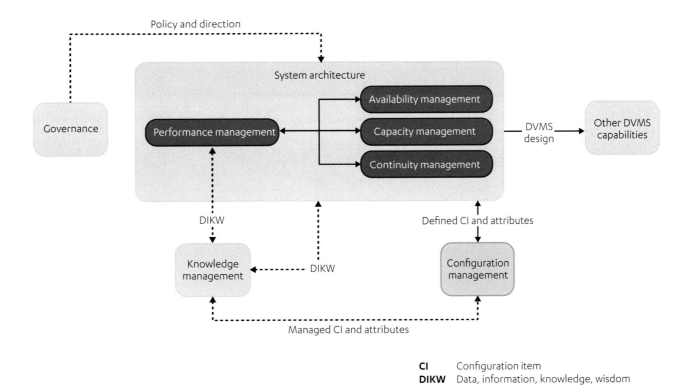

CI	Configuration item
DIKW	Data, information, knowledge, wisdom

Figure 5.7 Design: Capability overview

5.3.6.3 Change

Change is a fundamental organizational capability that enables the organization to adapt to its environment. The Change capability is driven by internal needs, external requirements, and a dynamic threat environment. It affects digital solutions that meet the design requirements necessary to create, protect, and deliver digital business value. It establishes the governance structure required to coordinate solutions that affect digital business value.

Practice areas (see Figure 5.8):

● Change coordination
● Solution adaptation
● Release management
● Deployment management.

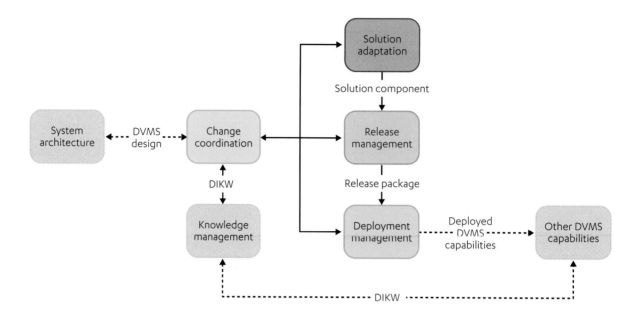

Figure 5.8 Change: Capability overview

5.3.6.4 Execute

The Execute capability represents the practice areas that create, protect, and deliver digital business value. These practice areas encompass providing access to digital products, services or systems to authorized users, mitigating disruptions in the delivery of digital business value, identifying and resolving systemic interruption or degradation of digital business value, and the overarching management of the infrastructure and platforms.

Practice areas (see Figure 5.9):

● Provisioning
● Incident management
● Problem management
● Infrastructure/platform management.

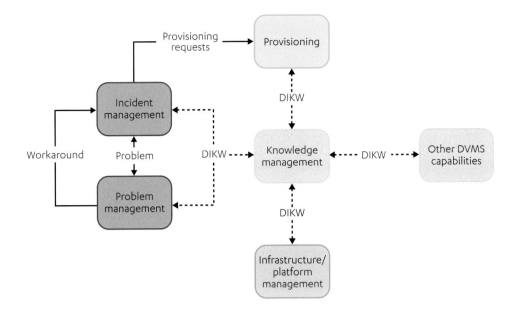

Figure 5.9 Execute: Capability overview

5.3.6.5   Innovate

The DVMS Model is an overlay of organizational capabilities that represent a minimum viable capability necessary for an organization to create, protect, and deliver digital business value. The model assumes the organization is at some unknown capability state. This approach marks the beginning of the journey to implement new cybersecurity capabilities or improve existing ones.

The organization must start where it is. It has no other choice. The CPD Model assumes a "current state" and that anything the organization does is an innovation of a given scope and impact. Innovation is "the introduction of something new." The CPD Model enables an organization to continually adapt to its current context through incremental or sustaining changes. It includes the capability of an organization to operationalize changes that are broader in scope and higher in the impact that may represent an adaptive or disruptive innovation.

The Innovate capability seeks opportunities for improving, creating, protecting, and delivering digital business value. The organizational context is the driver to achieve its expressed strategic and operational intent. It measures the overall performance of the components and systems that create, protect, and deliver digital business value, analyzes any performance gaps, and catalogs opportunities to innovate.

Much like a flywheel in a car engine provides mass that keeps the engine turning, continual innovation ensures that the DVMS capabilities adapt to the dynamic environmental context.

Practice areas (see Figure 5.10):

● Continual innovation
● Performance measurement
● Gap analysis.

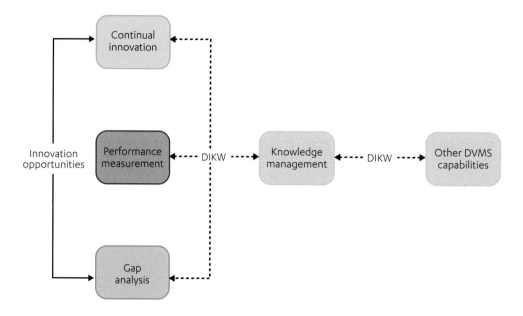

Figure 5.10 Innovate: Capability overview

The adopting and adapting organization can use the DVMS as an overlay representing the minimum viable capability to create, protect, and deliver digital business value to assess its current state. It can also adapt the DVMS to its context and use it to achieve its desired cybersecurity capabilities.

CHAPTER 6

Beyond the Framework?

6 Beyond the Framework?

An organization cannot just adopt the Framework, devoid of other considerations – the decision to adopt impacts the entire organization. Step zero, if you will, is acceptance by the most senior management (the board of directors or similar governing body) that the buck stops with them. The most high-ranking body must communicate the intent and work to get buy-in, rather than expecting decree to be sufficient to gain acceptance.

6.1   Before adopting the NIST-CSF

Adopting the NIST-CSF isn't the first step toward achieving the needed cybersecurity capabilities. The first step is an understanding that cybersecurity is *not* an information technology (IT) problem. The second step is to manage risk at the enterprise level and internalize the organization's capability to protect the value it creates. The third step requires understanding that adopting the NIST-CSF involves decisions about governance.

6.1.1   Cybersecurity is *not* an IT problem

It is hard to find an organization without a digital component fueled by information that supports real-time decision-making. Organizational agility is a requirement: it's no longer the idea that "the large eats the small"; now it's "the quick eats the slow." A business ecosystem leverages a network of suppliers and might also be a supplier.

With nearly every aspect of the enterprise dependent on digital technology, organizations have a massive cyber threat surface. The idea that cybersecurity is an IT problem is right out of the 1990s, yet 30 years later, organizations blindly delegate cybersecurity responsibility to IT without understanding board and executive management responsibility, and ultimately accountability when there is a breach. The bigger problem is grounded in the belief that cybersecurity is a technical problem, not a business problem.

6.1.2   Enterprise risk management starts at the top

Organizations must be adaptive to change. The ability to adapt requires the organization to incorporate explicit consideration of risk into the strategy development. The board has an oversight role in value creation, and is ultimately responsible not just for value creation but also for protecting business value. Consideration of performance risk becomes an ongoing exercise of integrating strategy and risk policies that support the organizational mission and vision. The resulting drive to achieve these business objectives puts the strategy into practice while serving as a basis for identifying, assessing, and responding to risk.

> *"When an organization elects, or fails, to put controls in place to mitigate the risk of loss or damage to their digital assets, they have effectively decided to self-insure for the exposure resulting from those omitted controls."*
> Ian W. Daykin, entrepreneur and business consultant

Enterprise risk management requires a continual process of obtaining and sharing necessary information from internal and external sources. It's not a matter of looking for this information – it already flows throughout the organization. As ERM practices evolve, the organization needs to maximize the business benefits, which requires the coordination of risk, compliance, process controls, and governance.

6.1.3　Adopting the NIST-CSF is about governance

A framework describes the "what and why" about a set of best practices within a knowledge domain: in our case, cybersecurity. Enterprise risk management and the resultant strategy and risk policies contribute to establishing management guidelines to adapt the NIST-CSF guidance and tailor its implementation to meet its internal needs, its external requirements, and a dynamic threat landscape. The actions resulting from developing these policy-based business objectives create business value and the appropriate value protection. This triggers changes to people's knowledge and skills, practices, processes and activities, and enabling technologies. The organization uses the DVMS as an informative reference overlay to assess the gaps and map a pathway to closing them.

Creating a culture of security

"The real purpose of cybersecurity awareness and training efforts should be to create a culture of security, meaning that employees should view good cybersecurity practices as good business and as part of 'how we do business here.' Employees should feel enabled to make good cybersecurity decisions and understand what makes a good decision. Awareness and training should focus on:

- "Stopping risky behavior: Help employees know what decisions can lead to a bad outcome. For example, opening email attachments from unknown sources

- "Encouraging less risky behavior: Help employees understand and care about implementing processes that increase security. For example, how to make strong passwords

- "Turning employees into sentinels: Help employees recognize and respond to a cybersecurity event. For example, what to do if a guest plugs an unauthorized USB drive into a machine."

Celia Paulsen (2020)

6.2　Getting ready to get ready

Before you start any journey, you have to prepare. You must understand that culture has to change to make cybersecurity a mission-critical capability. Begin by making it a program.

6.2.1　Cybersecurity – part of the organizational culture

Creating a cybersecurity culture is not an exercise in "touchy-feely" motivational meetings that are "once and done." Building a cybersecurity culture starts at the most senior levels of the organization and, with continual observable commitment, becomes woven into the fabric of the entire culture. It becomes "how we do things here."

Why is it challenging to create a cybersecurity culture? Let's start with buy-in. The people don't buy it, and the sad part is that this often includes a lack of executive buy-in. That is why we referred to "continual observable commitment" in the previous paragraph. Unless the executives accept that it is their problem, attempts to develop the appropriate culture devolve back to what was. Why? The employees see that the executives aren't walking the walk – the result is a "perfect storm" of ignorance and complacency.

For every complex problem, there is a simple, appealing solution that is wrong (to paraphrase H. L. Mencken). The easy approach is to make everyone attend a cybersecurity awareness lecture or take an online course. The executives pat themselves on the back for making everyone aware of cybersecurity while they continue to treat it as an IT problem. The employees consider it just another "flavor of the month."

"Cybersecurity is like owning a dog; it's a continual lifelong commitment."
David M. Nichols

In her Security Trails blog, Sara Jelen identified four ways to instill a cybersecurity culture (Jelen, 2019): [28]

- Start with the basics
- Engaging and ongoing cybersecurity training
- Use metrics to monitor post-training behaviors
- Make it easy to report threats.

6.2.1.1   Do basic stuff

Starting with the most basic cybersecurity policy, almost every organization has a password policy. Assuming it has one, are the employees aware of it, is it enforced, does it promote good password hygiene? What about access? Has the organization adopted the principle of least privilege? Do the employees know what they can access, and its importance to the business, and do they protect it from unauthorized access? What about two-factor authentication?

6.2.1.2   Cybersecurity training

Cybersecurity training is not a "once and done" exercise. It's not a matter of ticking a box, but putting together an inclusive cybersecurity training program (including board and executives), continual and relevant to each person's role – including contractors and consultants.

6.2.1.3   Measures and metrics

American automakers learned in the 1980s that it was impossible to inspect quality into a car. Crafting a quality car starts at the top; quality must be designed and built into the car and the processes to construct it, including the assembly line. Similarly, a cybersecurity program is only as effective as a cybersecurity culture. Tracking effectiveness and cybersecurity assessments must be outcome-based and relevant – not requirements-based. Outcomes provide value; requirements represent a list. Cybersecurity culture measures and metrics will change as the cybersecurity culture matures concurrently with the organizational cybersecurity capabilities.

---

28   A general approach to defining and changing organizational culture can be found in "The leader's guide to corporate culture" (Groysberg *et al.*, 2018).

6.2.1.4   See something, say something

A cybersecurity culture requires trust[29] that extends to the staff; a cyber-informed staff accepts responsibility to protect organizational digital assets. If people see something and report it through the appropriate channels, they trust it will result in appropriate action with no repercussions. It's not just accepting and acting on the report: trust requires the organization to encourage reporting. It's important to understand that all cybersecurity events have their genesis in a human failure. Open communication and trust with a cyber-informed staff will minimize things outside of software or hardware control.

6.2.1.5   Benefits of robust cybersecurity

Paul Frenken summed it up when he said:

> *"One of the best ways for an organization to reduce cyber risk is to build a culture of cybersecurity. This entails creating a mindset in employees that the risk is real and their daily actions impact that risk. Cybersecurity culture is important as it helps protect company assets from hardware to data. It needs to be part of a broader corporate culture of day-to-day actions that encourage employees to make thoughtful decisions that align with security policies. A security culture is more than just cybersecurity awareness. It requires the workforce to know the security risk and the process to avoid that risk. It's the building and enforcement of following an operating process of tasks that keeps the firm safe. Most organizations have spent years and countless resources to acquire and create their data asset, and if it is lost, stolen or corrupted, it could impact their bottom line for years to come."*
> (Frenken, 2020)

Everyone on staff (including full-time, part-time, and contractors) must clearly understand risk relative to the organization and their role within it. They must understand the impact they have in protecting organizational digital assets.

6.3   What do you do with what you know now?

The famous American philosopher Yogi Berra (Wikipedia, 2021i) once said, "When you come to a fork in the road, take it." When an organization finds itself at a cybersecurity "fork in the road," it can continue with the status quo or choose a path to robust cybersecurity capabilities based on effective enterprise risk management.

> *"Two basic rules of life are: 1) Change is inevitable. 2) Everybody resists change."*
> W. Edwards Deming

---

29   For more information on trust, see Stephen M. R. Covey's book *The Speed of Trust: The One Thing that Changes Everything* (Covey, 2008).

6.3.1   The "mission-vision" thing

Why start with the "mission-vision thing?" The simple answer is that cybersecurity is an enterprise problem, and it takes an enterprise-wide effort to mitigate it. The idea behind a mission-vision statement is to codify what the organization does and why it is essential. That is the *mission* statement. It establishes the "we are here" now. The *vision* paints a picture of where the organization is headed from the "here and now."

From the board to the loading dock (or high-tech equivalent), members of the organization should understand and summarize (not memorize) the mission statement (Fond, 2020) in about 25 to 30 words. Somewhere in that description, each organization member should clearly understand where they fit, how they contribute, and why.

The vision is forward-looking and paints a picture of a journey to a new and better future. Each organization member must envision where they will fit into the picture, how they will contribute, and why.

While that sounds like the "warm and fuzzy" stuff that I IR likes, the mission and vision play a critical role in shaping the organizational systems and behaviors. An organization whose culture is all about delivering on the mission and preparing for the future is one whose members become self-directed to achieve organizational goals and objectives. Integrating cybersecurity into the mission in support of the vision becomes an easy lift. Essentially, the organization can push decision-making closer to the activities that create and protect value.

6.3.2   Walking the walk – the executive team

Cybersecurity is a "business problem," not an "IT problem." The only way to address cybersecurity and make it "stick" is to start with senior management in the boardroom and executive suite (or governmental and military equivalent). The problem begins here, and only this management level can solve the problem.

Awareness of the cybersecurity problem is not equivalent to understanding the boardroom cybersecurity problem. Chapter 4 noted a 2012 report from the US Department of Homeland Security: a 52% increase in cybersecurity attacks on critical national infrastructure compared with 2011. Today it's worse. The world's critical infrastructure is under relentless cyberattack. Typically management, not just at organizations included in critical national infrastructure, lacks ERM expertise at the board level, leading to a struggle to appreciate and, therefore, understand the scope of the problem. The response led to the creation of the chief information security officer (CISO), which effectively fulfilled the same role as a goat in a tiger hunt.

The CISO was responsible for value protection, while the chief information officer (CIO) was responsible for value creation; the conflict between these perspectives doesn't help. Nobody is responsible for risk.

The answer isn't to fill the board or C-suite with tech-savvy members, but to formulate a strategic approach to ERM and articulate the role of cybersecurity in creating, protecting, and delivering digital business value.

"Walking the walk" is the term used when someone's actions back up their rhetoric. When the board internalizes ERM and the concept of protecting the value that the organization creates, guess what? The C-suite pays attention. When that happens, management and everyone else also takes notice as ERM and the creation and protection of value, combined with a structured approach to achieve the desired capabilities, cascade throughout the organization.

When the business acknowledges cybersecurity as a business problem, the entire organization mobilizes to create, protect, and deliver business value.

6.3.3   The journey and the commitment

The organization starts a journey when it chooses to create and protect value and adopt the NIST-CSF to mitigate its cybersecurity risks. The journey begins once the most senior management makes the strategic decision to adopt an enterprise risk management framework and the NIST-CSF Framework to mitigate cybersecurity risk.

The characteristics of this journey define an arc of a story that must answer the following questions:

- Where are we now?
- Where are we going?
- Why are we going?
- How will we handle the inevitable events that might occur that we didn't expect and for which we have no plan?
- How will we know we were successful?

The trek begins with establishing the organizational cybersecurity vision, articulating the reason for achieving better cybersecurity capabilities. No matter how well we plan, we know that unforeseen stuff happens. To respond to the unforeseeable, the journey to improve cybersecurity capabilities may encourage the organization to become more agile as it internalizes adapting to a rapidly changing environment while continually enhancing its capacity to create, protect, and deliver digital business value.

The organization demonstrates its commitment to the journey by what it says and does, including committing resources to the effort. The organization must devote its financial and intellectual capital to establishing a cybersecurity culture. The board or C-suite can't just phone this in. Full transparency and commitment are required.

Committing resources becomes easier if the organization links value creation with its protection. It also has another beneficial effect. If the organization treats value creation and protection as two sides of the same coin – inseparable from each other – this also potentially leads to changes in organizational behavior and structure. The organization funds value improvement; it funds creating and protecting value; it does not fund cybersecurity – it gets cybersecurity for free.

6.3.4   Pull the supply chain tight

Organizations exist in a complex ecosystem of interdependent business relationships. This "web" of organizations is connected via public and private networks. This connectedness and the interdependent nature of these relationships multiply the individual cybersecurity threat surfaces by every organization connected. In this web, the survival of each organization depends on the uninterrupted flow of information, its integrity, and its confidentiality.

> *"Think of the children's game of 'Pick-up-Sticks.'*
> *Everything is connected to everything else."*
> David M. Nichols

The cybersecurity capabilities of the supply chain are critical and must be part of the overall ERM strategy and an integral part of the cybersecurity program. Chapter 2 reviewed a pattern used to breach a large organization; the threat actor looked for and breached the weakest link in the supply chain.

The organization must engage its partners, up and downstream, as stakeholders in its cybersecurity outcomes. Establishing trust is essential. Validation and verification are required (trust but verify). Organizations in a supply chain share a common interest and overlapping threat landscapes, including multiple supply chains (at least one for each organization in the web) and common stakeholder interest in the associated cybersecurity programs.

6.3.5 Building the team

Improving or initiating a cybersecurity program requires a team. Legendary basketball coach John Wooden suggested an essential aspect of the necessary culture necessary for success when he said, "Make sure team members know they are working with you, not for you."

6.3.5.1 Program team structure

To understand how to build the cybersecurity program team, we need to start with the program's structure.

Figure 6.1 illustrates how the resources in the program team work together. The board or executive-level equivalent charters the cybersecurity program. An executive sponsor is appointed and is accountable to the board for program performance; the risk manager acts as an advisor. Depending on the size and complexity of the organization, it may have an entire executive-level risk team that supports the executive sponsor and program manager. The head auditor of the organization acts as an advisor to the program manager. The organization may also seek external support in the form of a program consultant and program trainers.

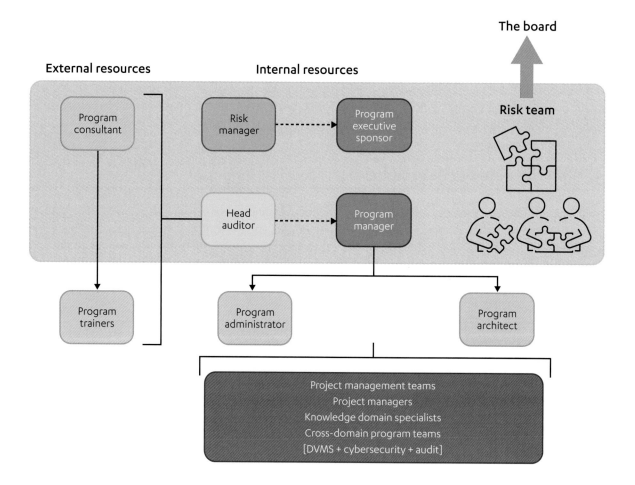

Figure 6.1 Using resources

The program architect and program administrator support the program manager. The program manager is responsible for program performance, and the program architect is accountable for the overall performance (including cybersecurity performance). The program manager oversees individual projects to implement or improve cybersecurity capabilities. The project teams require cross-domain knowledge specialists, DVMS and cybersecurity implementors, and internal auditors.

Notice the overall flow presented in this section. It starts with the most senior management establishing the strategy and governance requirements, which cascade through the rest of the organization in the form of operational management and execution.

6.3.5.2   The program team

There are seven key roles – roles do not equate to headcount – in the cybersecurity program team, as Figure 6.2 illustrates:

- **Program sponsor** Provides the executive leadership for the program. The sponsor is accountable to the board for the program outcomes and performance. The sponsor is advised by the executive team and risk management members. The sponsor actively participates in formulating risk-informed strategies. Direct managerial oversight is typically delegated to a senior-level manager to provide day-to-day program and project oversight.

- **Program manager** Has overall responsibility for the program objectives and the performance of the new and improved cybersecurity capabilities. The program manager has responsibility for the projects and works closely with the program architect to ensure the projects achieve the program's objectives.

- **Program architect** Responsible for the planning, design, change, execution, and innovation of the organization's capabilities to create, protect, and deliver digital business value. The architect works closely with the domain specialists, implementors, and internal auditors to ensure the achievement of the program's objectives.

- **Program administrator** Provides administrative support services to the program manager, program architect, and project administration. The administrator has budgetary oversight responsibility for the program.

- **Project manager** Responsible for achieving project objectives. The project manager has day-to-day responsibility for managing the project and its staff. An agile organization may apply a different name to this role, requiring a broader vision of the expected outcomes, focusing on priorities versus costs.

- **Implementor** A domain expert in the existing organizational DVMS or cybersecurity capabilities and controls. The implementor teams with other implementors and auditors to effect the cybersecurity project's outcome objectives: planning, design, change, execution, and innovation.

- **Auditor** Works as the program's internal auditor within the program or a project. The auditor works with the program architect, project manager, and team implementors to identify the instrumentation needed to produce the measures and metrics used to ensure that the DVMS capabilities are fit for use and purpose, and that the value delivered achieves the organization's strategic and operational intent.

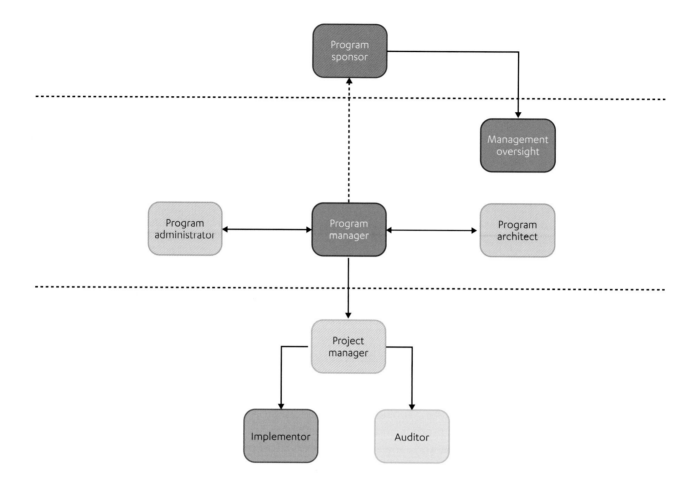

Figure 6.2 Cybersecurity program team

6.3.5.3 Investing in the team

An organization that chooses to adopt, adapt, and implement the guidance of the Framework must commit the necessary resources to achieve the desired cybersecurity outcomes. Investing in the training of the program and project staff is a must, as is providing role-appropriate cybersecurity training throughout the entire organization.

This kind of investment in training is not "once and done." The initial investment must be baked into the resource commitment to the cybersecurity program. Cyber awareness and capability training must become an ongoing investment to maintain cyberculture and ensure cyber capabilities evolve to keep pace with the changing environment and threat landscape.

The focus of this book is about enabling a "do it yourself" (DIY) approach for an adopting organization. Depending on its size and complexity, an adopting organization may outsource some or all cybersecurity programs. The staff responsible for executing and innovating cybersecurity capabilities must participate in the training program, with regularly updated course content.

"Cyber security risk management is a team sport built around an organization's people, practices, and technologies. The key to making it all work is to continually invest in training the technical and business workforce with the knowledge, skills, and capabilities for the creation, protection, and continual realization of digital business value."
Richard Lemieux

Continual innovation must become an organizational capability if the organization seeks to adapt its cybersecurity capabilities to meet its needs, its external requirements, and a dynamic threat landscape. Continual training and education go hand-in-glove with continual innovation.

6.4 What does "adoption" of the NIST-CSF look like?

What does the adoption of the NIST-CSF look like? This question is similar to the classic "What do you want to be when you grow up?" This section creates the vision of an organization and its journey.

6.4.1 Create, protect, and deliver value – a core or mission-critical organizational capability

The adoption of the Framework is a strategic decision. That decision carries a level of risk if the organization doesn't do it or fails in its adaptation and implementation.

6.4.1.1 Eyes wide open

In the context of the organizational ERM, the decision to adopt must be risk-informed as an integral part of the strategy to mitigate the cybersecurity risk. That strategic decision results in policies that form the management guidelines to:

● Create, protect, and deliver digital business value
● Establish measures and metrics for the organization's expressed strategic and operational intent
● Assure the performance of new or improved cybersecurity capabilities
● Assure the execution of strategic cybersecurity policies.

Any strategic decisions must answer the questions:

● "What are we doing?" – creating, protecting, and delivering digital business value
● "Why are we doing it?" – to assure the organization of the performance of new or improved cybersecurity capabilities
● "How will we do that?" – measure strategic and operational intent adequately to assure the effective and efficient execution of the strategic policies.

"Good intentions only count if you can prove you achieved them."
David M. Nichols

6.4.2   ERM and NIST-CSF – a structured approach to achieving your cybersecurity goals

Adopting an enterprise risk management framework provides the organizational imperative to adopt, adapt, and implement the Framework and its guidance to mitigate the organization's cyber risk. The broader scope of enterprise-wide risk management enables the organization to understand the role of cyber risk management in its formulation of risk-informed strategies. Enterprise risk management is the root of creating and protecting digital business value; it also internalizes organizational risk and rationalizes mitigation efforts.

An adopting organization will also create or improve its capability to continually innovate, improve, or sustain its cybersecurity capabilities while leveraging its agility to adapt to changing internal needs, external requirements, and a dynamic threat landscape. The adopting organization that operationalizes the CPD Model using the DVMS will use change (the ability to adapt) as a core or mission-critical organizational capability.

6.4.3   Loud and proud – commitment to success

Commitment to success requires trust that everyone works toward the organizational vision and mission. It also requires that every team member commit to learning and improving personally to contribute to team success. The weakest link is the individual who fails to improve and grow, improve existing skills, and learn new ones.

6.4.3.1   Who benefits?

The overall approach to adopting and adapting the Framework guidance requires the context of business value. The CPD Model enables the value an organization creates to be protected at a level commensurate with its value. Value is subjective, and it's what the "customer" says it is. Value also has a viewpoint: to whom is it valuable and why? Let's look at a shortlist of stakeholders.

- **The organization** Can create, protect, and deliver digital value, and it has become highly adaptable to changing needs and requirements, and a dynamic threat landscape
- **Customers** Can transact with the organization in a secure digital business environment where their information remains confidential, integral, and available
- **Supply chain partners** Can operate within a trusted environment where their information remains confidential, integral, and available
- **Critical-sector organizations** Can work together with a shared understanding of a structured approach to every member's cybersecurity capability to share and leverage best practices in a shared sector environment.

6.4.3.2   The target on your back

There is a zero chance that an organization will achieve 100% protection from all cybersecurity threats. That is why the Framework takes a risk-based approach. The adopting organization "sets the bar" for how much, and what types of, cybersecurity capability it needs. It is impossible to "comply" with a framework; compliance doesn't equate to being cyber secure. Review the information about the Target breach in Chapter 2: the company was "in compliance" and still suffered a significant breach. The Framework is not a "one-size-fits-all" approach for organizations seeking to implement or improve cybersecurity capabilities. However, it is a framework applicable to all organizations: public, private, military, etc.

An adopting organization will always have a target on its back. It's just the nature of existing in a world that leverages its digital assets to conduct business. The Framework isn't a "cloak of invisibility" either. Adopting and adapting the Framework makes that target on the organization's back smaller.

Another aspect that the Framework addresses is the constantly changing threat landscape and the internal organizational needs and external requirements: the organization must continually assess and adapt to its environment. Think of it as the quintessential "moving target."

6.4.3.3 Take control

Organizations today exist and operate in a hostile environment that includes a threat landscape, competitive pressures, and regulatory changes. That is a statement of fact, not a revelation. An organization that adopts, adapts, and implements the Framework guidance ceases to participate in the digital world passively. It chooses to take a proactive stance against cybersecurity threats through its risk-based approach to deploying the right cybersecurity capabilities it needs and continually adapting those capabilities to its current environment.

"Extinction is the rule. Survival is the exception."
Carl Sagan

Choose wisely.

Glossary

Glossary

adapt

In the NCSP scheme, "adapt" refers to the management decisions that result from the strategic governance decisions to "adopt" a framework or cybersecurity informative reference.

adopt

In the NCSP scheme, "adopt" refers to the strategic governance decision to select and apply a framework or cybersecurity informative reference.

AICPA

American Institute of Certified Public Accountants

attack vector

The way, means, or approach a bad or threat actor uses to gain potentially illegal access to computer systems.

Bloom's taxonomy

A hierarchical set of verbs that describes learning objectives.
https://www.bloomstaxonomy.net/

capability

In the systems engineering sense, "capability" is defined as the ability to execute a specified course of action. We also use it to aggregate one or more practice areas.
https://en.wikipedia.org/wiki/Capability_(systems_engineering)

CMS

The configuration management system (CMS) is a set of tools and data used to collect, store, manage, update, analyze, and present data about all configuration items and their relationships.

control

We define a generic control as part of a process that ensures repeatability. In cybersecurity, the control supports the identification, detection, protection, response, and recovery from a cybersecurity incident. Think of controls as requirements to produce or enable an outcome.

COSO

Committee of Sponsoring Organizations of the Treadway Commission

CPD Model

Create, protect, and deliver digital business value is the bottom layer of the DVMS, an abstraction or conceptualization of an organizational operating system.

CUI

Controlled Unclassified Information (CUI) is a category of unclassified information within the US Federal government. It is used extensively in NIST Special Publication (SP) 800-171.

culture

In an organization, culture is "the way we do things" based on the beliefs and attitudes that underlie the resulting behaviors.

CVE

Common Vulnerabilities and Exposures (CVE®) is a list of publicly disclosed cybersecurity vulnerabilities that is free to search, use, and incorporate into products and services.
https://cve.mitre.org/cve/

CVSS

The Common Vulnerability Scoring System (CVSS) is a free and open industry standard for assessing the severity of computer system security vulnerabilities. CVSS attempts to assign severity scores to vulnerabilities, allowing responders to prioritize responses and resources according to a threat. Scores are calculated based on a formula that depends on several metrics that approximate the ease of exploitation and its impact. Scores range from 0 to 10, with 10 being the most severe. While many utilize only the CVSS base score to determine severity, temporal and environmental scores also exist to factor in the availability of mitigations and how widespread vulnerable systems are within an organization.
https://en.wikipedia.org/wiki/Common_Vulnerability_Scoring_System

cybersecurity incident

If not addressed or resolved, a generic incident results in an unplanned negative impact on the business, including personal productivity. A cybersecurity incident is an incident with a cybersecurity origin.

DFARS

The Defense Federal Acquisition Regulation Supplement provides uniform acquisition policies for the US Department of Defense.
https://www.acq.osd.mil/DPAP/dars/dfarspgi/current/index.html

DIB

The Defense Industrial Base lists those companies that do business with the US Department of Defense. It includes both prime contractors and their associated subcontractors.

DVMS

The digital value management system (DVMS) is the overarching system that delivers digital value to stakeholders. It is composed of three adaptable and scalable layers: the DVMS, the Z-X Model, and the CPD Model. The DVMS is a "black box" to the outside world. It overlays what the organization does and how it produces outcomes for stakeholders. The Z-X Model includes seven core organizational capabilities (Govern/Governance, Assure/Assurance, Plan, Design, Change, Execute, and Innovate). The CPD Model operationalizes the Z-X Model.

ERM

Enterprise risk management (ERM) in business includes the methods and processes used by organizations to manage risks and seize opportunities related to achieving their objectives.
https://en.wikipedia.org/wiki/Enterprise_risk_management

ERM framework

A framework for risk management. In this context, a framework describes what to do, not how.

escalation archetype

An escalation archetype is part of the visual language of systems thinking. The escalation archetype system can be described using causal loop diagrams that consist of balancing and reinforcing loops.
https://en.wikipedia.org/wiki/Escalation_archetype

FastTrack™

A structured approach to adapt the NIST-CSF and one or more of its informative references. It provides rapid adaptation, implementation, operation, and improvement of the relevant cybersecurity control families. FastTrack™ addresses adaptation following the strategic decision to adopt the NIST-CSF.

governance

The processes of interaction and decision-making among the actors involved in a collective problem that lead to the creation, reinforcement, or reproduction of social norms and institutions.
https://arcticyearbook.com/arctic-yearbook/2015/2015-preface

GQM

Goal, question, metric (GQM) is an established goal-oriented approach to software metrics to improve and measure software quality.
https://en.wikipedia.org/wiki/GQM

hacktivist

A computer hacker with a social or political cause.

HIDS

A host-based intrusion detection system (HIDS) runs on an individual host or device on the network. A HIDS monitors the inbound and outbound packets from a device and only alerts the user or administrator if suspicious activity is detected.
https://en.wikipedia.org/wiki/Intrusion_detection_system

informative reference

Informative references are citations of detailed cybersecurity documents to any combination of functions, categories, and subcategories within the NIST-CSF. Informative references demonstrate how a given cybersecurity document can be used in coordination with the framework for cybersecurity risk management.
https://www.nist.gov/cyberframework/informative-references

ISO/IEC 27000

The ISO/IEC 27000 series comprises information security standards published jointly by the International Organization for Standardization (ISO) and the International Electrotechnical Commission (IEC).
https://en.wikipedia.org/wiki/ISO/IEC_27000-series

malware

A portmanteau of malicious software. It is intended to damage or disable computers and computer systems.
https://en.wikipedia.org/wiki/Malware

misuse case

The term "misuse case" case is derived from and is the inverse of "use case". It describes executing a malicious act against a system, while a use case describes any action taken by the system.
https://en.wikipedia.org/wiki/Misuse_case

model

An abstracted pattern of behaviors that supports understanding or replicating a set of processes, activities, or tasks.

NIDS

A network intrusion detection system (NIDS) is placed at a strategic point (or points) within the network to monitor traffic to and from all devices on the network. It performs an analysis of passing traffic on the entire subnet and matches the traffic that passes on the subnet to the library of known attacks.
https://en.wikipedia.org/wiki/Intrusion_detection_system

NIST

The National Institute of Standards and Technology (NIST) is part of the US Department of Commerce, and is one of the oldest physical science laboratories in the US.
https://www.nist.gov/

NIST SP 800-39

The full title of this publication is *Managing Information Security Risk: Organization, Mission, and Information System View.*
https://nvlpubs.nist.gov/nistpubs/Legacy/SP/nistspecialpublication800-39.pdf

NIST SP 800-53

The full title of this publication is *Security and Privacy Controls for Information Systems and Organizations.*
https://csrc.nist.gov/publications/detail/sp/800-53/rev-5/final

NIST SP 800-171

The full title of this publication is *Protecting Controlled Unclassified Information in Nonfederal Systems and Organizations.*
https://csrc.nist.gov/publications/detail/sp/800-171/rev-2/final

PCI DSS

The Payment Card Industry Data Security Standard (PCI DSS) is an information security standard for organizations that handle branded credit cards from the major card schemes. The PCI DSS is mandated by the card brands but administered by the Payment Card Industry Security Standards Council. The Standard was created to increase controls around cardholder data, thereby reducing credit card fraud.

PDSA

Plan Do Study Adjust (PDSA; also Plan Do Check Act or PDCA) comes from the work of W. Edwards Deming; it is a systematic cycle for learning to continually improve a product, process, or service. PDSA is an updated version.
https://deming.org/explore/pdsa/

phishing

Phishing is the fraudulent attempt to obtain sensitive information or data, such as usernames, passwords, credit card details, or other sensitive details, by impersonating oneself as a trustworthy entity in digital communication.
https://en.wikipedia.org/wiki/Phishing

PMO

A program or project management office (PMO) is responsible for defining and maintaining program or project management standards across an organization.

practice

Practices aggregate one or more processes that accomplish how an organization does things.

practice area

Groups of practices that describe what an organization does – not how.

principle

An immutable proposition or value that is a guide for behavior or evaluation.
https://en.wikipedia.org/wiki/Principle

process

A set of activities designed to accomplish an objective, with appropriate controls to ensure repeatability at producing the desired outcome.

program management

The process of managing several related projects.

project management

Projects introduce change. Project management is the process of leading the work of a team to achieve the project's goals and meet the success criteria at a specified time.
https://en.wikipedia.org/wiki/Project_management

QO–QM

Question Outcome–Question Metric (QO–QM) is an adaptation of the GQM+Strategies® to fit the CPD Model.

ransomware

A type of malware that encrypts organizational data and systems until and unless a ransom is paid. The attackers may also threaten the victim with data exposure unless the ransom is paid – also known as extortion.
https://en.wikipedia.org/wiki/Ransomware

risk appetite

Risk appetite is the level of risk that an organization is prepared to accept before action is deemed necessary to reduce the risk.
https://en.wikipedia.org/wiki/Risk_appetite

risk management

Risk management is the identification, evaluation, and prioritization of risks (defined in ISO 31000 as the effect of uncertainty on objectives) followed by the coordinated and economic application of resources to minimize, monitor, and control the probability or impact of unfortunate events or to maximize the realization of opportunities.
https://en.wikipedia.org/wiki/Risk_management

SOA

The statement of applicability (SOA) is one of the required documents for ISO 27001 compliance/certification. The document lists all of the controls in Annex A and details if they are included or excluded, with appropriate justification and information about their implementation.

strategy

A strategy forms the basis for the choices that underlie the system that delivers value via the DVMS.

system

A system is a group of interrelated and interacting parts that are organized to accomplish a purpose. The parts that make up the "whole" have the following characteristics:

- Each part affects the behavior or properties of the whole
- Each part of the system, when it acts within or impacts the system, is dependent on the effect of some other part
- No part of a system (or collection of parts) has an independent effect
- A system is not the sum of its parts – it is the product of interactions between the parts.

ISO/IEC/IEEE defines a system as follows: "A system (combines) interacting elements organized to achieve one or more stated purposes. The interacting elements that compose a system include hardware, software, data, humans, processes, procedures, facilities, materials, and naturally occurring entities."
https://www.iso.org/standard/63711.html

system archetype

System archetypes are patterns of behavior of a system. Systems expressed by circles of causality have, therefore, similar structures.
https://en.wikipedia.org/wiki/System_archetype

systems thinking

An approach to examining and understanding complex systems by looking at the whole. The performance of a system depends on the interactions of the elements within the system. Each actor within a system has its own unique perspective of the system.

tension metrics

Metrics that attempt to balance three or more related and competing metrics.

threat actor

In computer security, a threat is a potential adverse action or event that has been facilitated by a vulnerability, resulting in an unwanted impact on a computer system or application. A threat actor is an entity that carries out this action.

threat landscape

A threat landscape is a collection of threats in a particular domain or context, with information on identified vulnerable assets, threats, risks, threat actors, and observed trends.
https://itlaw.wikia.org/wiki/Threat_landscape

use case

A list of actions or event steps that defines the interactions between a role (or actor) and a system to achieve a goal.
https://en.wikipedia.org/wiki/Use_case

value

The perceived benefit of something. It is the customer or user who determines the value of something.

value stream

A series of activities that creates a flow of value to the customer (i.e., the product or service).

vishing

Voice phishing or vishing is a form of criminal phone fraud that uses social engineering over the telephone system to gain access to private personal and financial information for monetary gain.
https://en.wikipedia.org/wiki/Voice_phishing

VPN

A virtual private network (VPN) provides privacy, anonymity, and security to users by creating a private network across a public network.
https://en.wikipedia.org/wiki/Virtual_private_network

Z-X Model

The Z-X Model is part of the DVMS. It represents the high-level aspect of the DVMS that executes a strategy. The objective is to recognize and action a value gap. The Z-X Model includes a common set of capability-flows across multiple DVMS adaptations. It defines seven organizational capabilities: Govern/Governance, Assure/Assurance, Plan, Design, Change, Execute, and Innovate. Governance addresses the oversight of organizational control and direction. Assurance addresses the confidence in the efficiency and effectiveness of execution.

References

References

Android Authority (2021). The first camera phone was sold 22 years ago, and it's not what you'd expect. https://www.androidauthority.com/first-camera-phone-anniversary-993492/.

Basili, V., Trendowicz, A., Kowalczyk, M., Heidrich, J., Seaman, C., Münch, J., and Rombach, D. (2014). Aligning Organizations Through Measurement: The GQM+Strategies Approach. Springer, New York.

Carnegie Mellon University (2017). CERT Insider Threat Center. https://resources.sei.cmu.edu/library/asset-view.cfm?assetid=91513.

CISA (n.d.). Information sharing and analysis organizations (ISAOs). https://www.cisa.gov/information-sharing-and-analysis-organizations-isaos.

Cisco (n.d.). What is a cyberattack? https://www.cisco.com/c/en/us/products/security/common-cyberattacks.html.

The Clever (2017). 15 huge supercomputers that were less powerful than your smartphone. https://www.theclever.com/15-huge-supercomputers-that-were-less-powerful-than-your-smartphone/.

CNBC (2017). Watch this Russian hacker break into our computer in minutes (YouTube video). https://www.youtube.com/watch?v=CV39QzFpJx4.

CNBC (2021a). Why the U.S. can't stop cyber attacks (YouTube video). https://www.youtube.com/watch?v=hSQf3hUx9J0.

CNBC (2021b). 'Zero-day' cyber attacks are destructive, becoming more common: expert (YouTube video). https://www.youtube.com/watch?v=4F4L6WgB7Rg.

COSO (2013). COSO Internal Control – Integrated Framework: Executive Summary, Framework and Appendices, and Illustrative Tools for Assessing Effectiveness of a System of Internal Control (3 volume set). AICPA. https://www.coso.org/Documents/990025P-Executive-Summary-final-may20.pdf.

COSO (2017). Enterprise risk management: Integrating with strategy and performance – Executive summary. https://www.coso.org/Documents/2017-COSO-ERM-Integrating-with-Strategy-and-Performance-Executive-Summary.pdf.

COSO (2019). Managing cyber risk in a digital age. https://www.coso.org/Documents/COSO-Deloitte-Managing-Cyber-Risk-in-a-Digital-Age.pdf.

Covey, S. M. R. (2008). *The Speed of Trust: The One Thing that Changes Everything*. Free Press, New York.

Covey, S. R. (2004). *The 7 Habits of Highly Effective People: Powerful Lessons in Personal Change*. Free Press, New York.

Deming, W. E. (2000). *Out of the Crisis*. MIT Press, Cambridge, MA.

Drucker, P. F. (1973). *Management: Tasks, Responsibilities, Practices*. Harper & Row, New York.

Drucker, P. F. (1985). *Innovation and Entrepreneurship: Practice and Principles*. Harper & Row, New York.

Drucker, P. F. (1999). *Management Challenges for the 21st Century*, 1st edition. HarperBusiness, New York.

Exabeam (2019). Creeper: The world's first computer virus. https://www.exabeam.com/information-security/creeper-computer-virus/.

Expert Program Management (2018). Mintzberg's 5 Ps of strategy. https://expertprogrammanagement.com/2018/04/5-ps-of-strategy/.

FBI (2018). The Morris Worm: 30 years since first major attack on the internet.
https://www.fbi.gov/news/stories/morris-worm-30-years-since-first-major-attack-on-internet-110218.

FBI (2020). *Internet Crime Report 2020*.
https://www.ic3.gov/Media/PDF/AnnualReport/2020_IC3Report.pdf.

Fond (2020). Best mission statements: 12 examples you need to see.
https://www.fond.co/blog/best-mission-statements/.

Frenken, P. (2020). Why build a cybersecurity culture? (ISACA blog post).
https://www.isaca.org/resources/news-and-trends/isaca-now-blog/2020/why-build-a-cybersecurity-culture.

Freund, J., and Jones, J. (2015). *Measuring and Managing Information Risk: A FAIR Approach*. Elsevier BH, Amsterdam.

Groysberg, B., Lee, J., Price, J., and Cheng, J. Y-J. (2018). The leader's guide to corporate culture. *Harvard Business Review* Jan.–Feb. 2018. Reprint number R1801B.

History Computer (2021). TCP/IP - Complete History of the TCP/IP Protocol Suite.
https://history-computer.com/tcp-ip-complete-history-of-the-tcp-ip-protocol-suite/.

IBM (2017). A brief history of cloud computing.
https://www.ibm.com/cloud/blog/cloud-computing-history.

Infosec (2016). The breach of Anthem Health – the largest healthcare breach in history.
https://resources.infosecinstitute.com/topic/the-breach-of-anthem-health-the-largest-healthcare-breach-in-history/.

Jelen, S. (2019). Cyber security culture: Why it matters for your business.
https://securitytrails.com/blog/cybersecurity-culture.

Kaspersky (2016). Malware: Difference between computer viruses, worms and Trojans (YouTube video).
https://www.youtube.com/watch?v=n8mbzU0X2nQ.

Mandiant (2020). SUNBURST additional technical details.
https://www.mandiant.com/resources/sunburst-additional-technical-details.

McCumber, C. (2009). What kind of thinker am I? Linear vs. Non-linear thinking.
https://chuckslamp.com/index.php/2009/04/11/non-linearthinking/#:~:text=Non%2Dlinear%20thought%20increases%20possible,they%20have%20the%20most%20interest.

NCSC (2021). Protecting critical and emerging US technologies from foreign threats.
https://www.dni.gov/index.php/ncsc-newsroom/item/2254-ncsc-fact-sheet-protecting-critical-and-emerging-u-s-technologies-from-foreign-threats.

Netwrix (2018). Top 10 most common types of cyber attacks.
https://blog.netwrix.com/2018/05/15/top-10-most-common-types-of-cyber-attacks/.

Neumann, von J. (1966). Theory of Self-Reproducing Automata. Available at
https://cba.mit.edu/events/03.11.ASE/docs/VonNeumann.pdf.

NIST (2018). Framework for Improving Critical Infrastructure Cybersecurity, Version 1.1.
https://nvlpubs.nist.gov/nistpubs/cswp/nist.cswp.04162018.pdf.

NITTF (n.d.). Mission Fact Sheet.
https://www.dni.gov/files/NCSC/documents/products/National_Insider_Threat_Task_Force_Fact_Sheet.pdf.

OWASP (n.d.). OWASP Top Ten. Accessed Jan. 12, 2022.
https://owasp.org/www-project-top-ten/.

Paulsen, C. (2020). Creating a culture of security.
https://www.qualitydigest.com/inside/operations-article/creating-culture-security-102720.html.

Perlroth, N. (2021). *This Is How They Tell Me the World Ends: The Cyber Weapons Arms Race*. Bloomsbury Publishing, London.

Pingdom (2010). 15 fantastic firsts on the Internet. https://www.pingdom.com/blog/15-fantastic-firsts-on-the-internet/.

Privacy Risks Advisors (2017). A new in-depth analysis of Anthem breach. https://www.privacyrisksadvisors.com/news/a-new-in-depth-analysis-of-anthem-breach/.

Risk Based Security (2014). A breakdown and analysis of the December, 2014 Sony hack. https://www.riskbasedsecurity.com/2014/12/05/a-breakdown-and-analysis-of-the-december-2014-sony-hack/.

Rose, S. W., Borchert, O., Mitchell S., and Connelly, S. (2020). Zero trust architecture (NIST Special Publication). https://www.nist.gov/publications/zero-trust-architecture.

SANS Institute (2014). Case study: Critical controls that could have prevented target breach. https://www.sans.org/white-papers/35412/.

SANS Institute (2015a). Case study: Critical controls that Sony should have implemented. https://www.sans.org/white-papers/36022/.

SANS Institute (2015b). Case study: The Home Depot data breach. https://www.sans.org/white-papers/36367/.

SANS Institute (2021). SolarWinds – a SANS Lightning Summit recap. https://www.sans.org/blog/solarwinds-sans-lightning-summit-recap/.

Senge, P. M. (1990). *The Fifth Discipline: The Art and Practice of the Learning Organization* (1st ed.). Doubleday, New York.

Senge, P. M. (2006). *The Fifth Discipline: The Art and Practice of the Learning Organization* (2nd ed.). Penguin Random House, New York.

TOP500 (n.d.). No. 1 system in June 1994. https://www.top500.org/resources/top-systems/intel-xps-140-paragon-sandia-national-labs/.

Verizon (n.d.). 2021 Data Breach Investigations Report. Accessed Jan. 12, 2022. https://www.verizon.com/business/resources/reports/dbir/.

Wikipedia (2021a). Advanced persistent threat. Last modified Dec. 9, 2021. https://en.wikipedia.org/wiki/Advanced_persistent_threat.

Wikipedia (2021b). CDC 6600. Last modified Dec. 12, 2021. https://en.wikipedia.org/wiki/CDC_6600.

Wikipedia (2021c). History of the World Wide Web. Last modified Dec. 9, 2021. https://en.wikipedia.org/wiki/History_of_the_World_Wide_Web.

Wikipedia (2021d). Root cause analysis. Last modified Dec. 10, 2021. https://en.wikipedia.org/wiki/Root_cause_analysis.

Wikipedia (2021e). SolarWinds. Last modified Nov. 4, 2021. https://en.wikipedia.org/wiki/SolarWinds.

Wikipedia (2021f). Steven Sasson. Last modified Nov. 15, 2021. https://en.wikipedia.org/wiki/Steven_Sasson.

Wikipedia (2021g). Transistor. Last modified Dec. 30, 2021. https://en.wikipedia.org/wiki/Transistor.

Wikipedia (2021h). UNIVAC I. Last modified Dec. 19, 2021.
https://en.wikipedia.org/wiki/UNIVAC_I.

Wikipedia (2021i). Yogi Berra. Last modified Dec. 2, 2021.
https://en.wikipedia.org/wiki/Yogi_Berra.

Wikipedia (2022a). ARPANET. Last modified Jan. 10, 2022.
https://en.wikipedia.org/wiki/ARPANET.

Wikipedia (2022b). Computer virus. Last modified Jan. 11, 2022.
https://en.wikipedia.org/wiki/Computer_virus.

Wikipedia (2022c). Edward Snowden. Last modified Jan. 11, 2022.
https://en.wikipedia.org/wiki/Edward_Snowden.

Wikipedia (2022d). Electrical telegraph. Last modified Jan. 6, 2022.
https://en.wikipedia.org/wiki/Electrical_telegraph.

Wikipedia (2022e). History of computing hardware (1960s–present). Last modified Jan. 9, 2022.
https://en.wikipedia.org/wiki/History_of_computing_hardware_(1960s%E2%80%93present).

Wikipedia (2022f). History of the Internet. Last modified Jan. 3, 2022.
https://en.wikipedia.org/wiki/History_of_the_Internet.

Wikipedia (2022g). Internet of things. Last modified Jan. 3, 2022.
https://en.wikipedia.org/wiki/Internet_of_things.

Wikipedia (2022h). Moore's law. Last modified Jan. 10, 2022.
https://en.wikipedia.org/wiki/Moore%27s_law.

Wikipedia (2022i). Project Xanadu. Last modified Jan. 1, 2022.
https://en.wikipedia.org/wiki/Project_Xanadu.

WIRED (2015). Hackers remotely kill a jeep on a highway (YouTube video).
https://www.youtube.com/watch?v=MK0SrxBC1xs.

Scan the QR code to access the list of references at
www.tsoshop.co.uk/adopting-nist-csf-references

Index

Index